Going Against the Tide

PROPHETICALLY

Of all the biblical doctrines to be searched out, eschatology is, by far, the most complex. There are seven principal views, five involving a rapture at some point in time and two rejecting the idea altogether. This book is written from the pre-tribulation rapture viewpoint. It is not so much a defense of this view as it is an assessment of the multitude of events, characters, and meanings (or purposes) of these events. Is the author's persuasion that there should be many corrections made, not to the framework but to the many details of this view. This book is original, and it includes many corrections and alterations to some long-held views. The reader is urged to search the Scriptures without biases to see whether these things are so.

This is the author's first (and maybe last) book written at a time in life when most people are either in retirement or anticipating it. But with well over 57 years of searching Scripture and with his graduation from the evening school division of Philadelphia College of Bible (now CAIRN University) over thirty years ago, he felt that the accumulated knowledge of all those years should be shared with others. It is left up to the reader to decide whether this "elder" has been led astray by evil powers or perhaps by his own imagination, or whether the Spirit of God has illuminated (not inspired) his mind in his search for truth.

Going Against the Tide

PROPHETICALLY

AN ASSESSMENT OF CURRENT TEACHINGS FROM THE PRE-TRIBULATION VIEWPOINT

WALTER MADENFORD

ReadersMagnet, LLC

FOREWORD

I f the reader is not quite familiar with Bible prophecy then the following Scriptures should be read at least three times in three different translations. Suggested translations: King James Version (KJV), New King James Version (NKJV), New American Standard Bible (NASB), Amplified Bible. The following are the principal Scriptures used but not the only ones.

Ez.20:33 - 38 and chapters 36 through 39

Dan. 2;7;8;9:24 - 27; 11::21 - 45; 12

Joel chapters 1 through 3

Zech. Chapters 12; 13; 14

Matt. Chapters 13:3-9, 18-33, 36-50; 24;25

Mark 13

Luke 17:20 - 37; 21:5 - 36

John 14:1 - 3

Acts 2:14 - 21; 15:13 - 17

1 Thes. 4:13 - 5:11

2 Thes. 2:1 - 12

1 Tim. 4:1 - 5

2 Tim. 3:1 - 9

James 5:1 - 9

2 Pet. 3:3 - 13

1 John 2:18 - 22

Rev. Chapters 6; 7:9-17; 8; 9; 11; 12; 13; 14:17-20; 16; 17; 18; 19; 20:1-10

PREFACE

Many books have been written on the subject of prophecy. Several magazines and ministries are almost exclusively devoted to this subject. The subject is so vast that seldom does an author attempt to cover the entire subject. This book, like most others, will attempt to cover the entire subject. This book, like most others, will attempt to deal with certain portions of the prophetic picture. Prophetic studies must necessarily begin in ancient times and proceed down to the climax of history.

Those who have ventured into the subject of prophecy somewhat extensively must have noticed the many different views, some with major differences, some with minor differences. This book is written from the pre-tribulation (rapture) position. During the decades of my searching the Scriptures, I have become persuaded of the need for change in many of the details of this position. One might ask, "Does it really matter?" I think so. It appears there may be a reward for those who get things right; "Those who are wise shall shine like the brightness of the firmament" (Daniel 12:13).

CONTENTS

CHAPTER 1

PRE-TRIBULATION RAPTURE –
VIEWS GENERALLY HELD

Those who take the prophetic Scriptures literally believe there will be a millennial (1000 year) reign of Christ at the end of this present age. The term pre-millennial refers to events occurring just prior to this millennial reign. There are five basic pre-millennial positions. They refer to the time of the rapture relative to a seven-year period preceding the millennium. This seven-year period has been referred to as the tribulation period. They are as follows:

1. Pre-tribulation rapture - the view that the rapture occurs just before the tribulation period.

2. Mid-tribulation rapture - the view that the rapture occurs in the middle of this period.

3. Pre-wrath rapture - the view that the rapture occurs sometime in the last half of this period.

4. Post-tribulation rapture - the view that the rapture occurs at the end of this period.

5. Partial rapture - same as pre-tribulation rapture except that all the saints are not included.

These views have several differences but also have many things in common. Many authors have attempted to defend these various views. Even within one particular view various scenarios have been set forth. This book is an attempt to set forth what the author believes to be the correct scenario for the pre-tribulation rapture view.

There are many characters and events involved in this teaching and we must go back in time, at least to the time of the Babylonian Empire, to get a full picture. There were other nations prior to the rise of the Babylonian Empire who fought against Israel but it was at the time of the Babylonian captivity that the times of the Gentiles started. In the second chapter of Daniel we read of successive kingdoms following Babylon. First was the Medo-Persian kingdom, then the Grecian, followed by Christ to establish His kingdom, but it should be noted that the characteristics of this empire seem to change somewhat at the latter end. This has given rise to the "revived Roman Empire" idea. It should be noted at this point that during the Grecian Empire there is considerable mention made of an evil king named Antiochus Epiphanes who invaded Israel, slaughtered many Jews and desecrated the temple. Here we first read that infamous expression "abomination of desolation." This expression is also applied to the antichrist at the end of the age who will duplicate those evil actions of Antiochus. Because of the striking resemblance of the two, many expositors have taken verses referring to Antiochus and have applied them to the antichrist. They consider Antiochus to be a type or picture of the coming antichrist. Is this authors view there is more to it than that.

In the seventh chapter of Daniel there are four beats described. The standard interpretation of this equates these beasts (kingdoms) to the same kingdoms described in the second chapter of Daniel, i.e. Babylon, Persia, Greece, and Rome. I will take exception to this later. In the ninth chapter of Daniel we have a prophecy (a key prophetic passage) relating to the nation of Israel. It is the well known seventy weeks (70 X 7 = 490 years) prophecy which details the future of Israel, beginning with the rebuilding of Jerusalem, and for 69 weeks (483 weeks) Israel rebuilds in troublous times, is invaded, persecuted, again drives out her enemies and enters the time of Roman rule. The 483 years ends with the crucifixion of Christ. There is then a prophecy of the second destruction of Jerusalem and an extended time period of desolation and war. An astonishing thing happens in the last verse. Without any explanation we read of a "prince shall come" confirming a covenant with Israel and many others, and then putting a stop to sacrifices and offering in the "middle of the week." Reading between the lines we realize the Jews have come back to their land, rebuilt their temple, begun their sacrificial system again, apparently in the first half of the week (3 & 1/2 years). It is evident from this that there is a time break between the 69th and 70th week. It is this 70th week, particularly the last half of it, that much of end-time prophecy deals with.

There is much agreement among expositors that the Roman Empire will be revived. Not only is it indicated in the second chapter of Daniel but it is also implied in the ninth chapter as well. Since the "prince shall come" is said to be from the empire that is responsible for the destruction of the second temple, and we know from history that it was the Roman legions who were responsible for this, then the "prince shall come" must come from Rome. We read in Daniel 11 and Revelation 6 of the wars of conquest of the future Roman ruler. Many expositors believe the "prince that shall come" will be the future beast or antichrist. But there is another side to this. In Ezekiel 38 & 39 we read of other nations attacking Israel in the "latter days." A coalition of nations headed by Gog and Magog - probably Russia according to most commentators

—invades Israel. Most expositors put the attack by Gog and Magog before the wars of the antichrist heading up the revived Roman Empire. This raises many questions.

There are many events, characters, and nations involved in the end time prophecy. In Daniel 11 we read of the antichrist fighting (and apparently conquering) nations from the north, south, and the east - but not from the west. But we also read about the "kings of the east" in Revelation 16 coming toward Israel for the battle of Armageddon. When antichrist fights against the nations from the north does this include Gog and Magog whose armies were totally defeated by God Himself? Some manuscripts say that the sixth part of those armies were left, other manuscripts say that all were destroyed. In Revelation 9, under the sixth trumpet judgment, we read about an army of two hundred million "horsemen" destroying a third of mankind. Later in Revelation 16 where the kings of the east are described expositors attempt to equate these "horsemen" with the armies coming from that area. These are two different judgments, one on the sixth trumpet judgment, the other the sixth bowl judgment.

Another entity well worth mentioning is the "harlot" in Revelation 17 & 18 (there is also a preview of her in Revelation !4:8_. she is evidently a religious and commercial "harlot." Her influence, wealth, and destruction are vividly described. The 10 kings of the revived, or reviving, Roman Empire hate the harlot, give their authority to the beast, who then destroys the harlot. The timing of this event poses problems for expositors. Is it at the beginning, the middle, or near the end of the 70th week. There seems to be general agreement that the 70th week is an unbroken period of 7 years.

Some characters in the end time scenario are: the beast, false prophet, an image that speaks (demonic activity, no doubt), two witnesses, 1,440,000 Jews - servants of God, perhaps witnesses, a multitude of martyred Gentile converts, the devil, various angelic and demonic beings, part of the nation of Israel described as a woman, and Christ returning with His saints at Armageddon. As stated before many consider the coming Roman prince and the beast to be the same person.

The two witnesses are a subject of controversy; their identity and their time of service are two areas of dispute. One is certain to be Elijah for this is predicted in Malachi 4:5. the other is either Moses or Enoch. Moses was picked because the judgments occurring under their period of witnessing are quite similar to those which occurred in Egypt. Also, Moses appeared with Elijah on the mount of transfiguration. Enoch was picked because he, like Elijah, was translated and did not die. Both of them are slain here. Also he was the first person to prophesy of the coming of the Lord with His saints in judgment. Some feel he would represent the Gentiles and Elijah would represent Israel; however, their area of witnessing seems to be confined to Israel Concerning the time of their witnessing, some think the first half of the 70th week, others think the second half. Majority view appears to be the first half.

The person getting the most attention in any study of end time prophecy is certainly the antichrist, or beast, of Revelation 13. Associated with him is the false prophet and a speaking (demon controlled) image. He is said to be a resurrected individual. Some do not take this literally and apply it to the Roman Empire rather than to the beast himself. Most expositors seem to favor the literal interpretation. In Revelation 6:1 we read about an individual with a bow on a white horse going out conquering and to conquer. There is almost universal agreement this person is the beast starting out on his goal of the world conquest and self deification. A few believe this person is Christ but that doesn't fit with the context. Various views about the identification of the beast have been set forth. Many see him as the Roman Prince of Daniel 9:26. Others see him as an Islamic (Islamic beast theory) and an apostate Pope as the false prophet. One author sees him as a resurrected Adolph Hitler. His number - 666 - has been the subject of much speculation but doesn't seem to help much to identify him. Those who take the resurrection prophecy literally place his resurrection either in the early part of the 70th week or at about the middle. Revelation 17 sheds more light on the identification (or origination) of the beast. A beast with 7 heads and 10 horns is described there. The 10 horns are 10 future kings of the revived Roman Empire. The 7 heads are 7 kings of 7 successive kingdoms in history- past, present and future. We are then told there is an eighth king who is "out of the seven" this eighth king is the beast. More will be said about this in a later chapter.

In Revelation 12 there is a woman mentioned who is obviously the nation- or rather, part of the nation - of Israel. She is said to flee into the wilderness to a place prepared for her, where she will be taken care of for 3 1/2 years. She will flee there to escape the wrath of the serpent (the Devil) who is trying to persecute (or destroy) her. This ties in with the Olivet discourse of Matthew 24 where Jews living in Judea at the end time are told to flee to the mountains when the abomination of desolation is set up. This occurs at the middle of the week. Many have speculated about where the Jews will flee, and majority opinion is a place called Petra in southern Palestine, where the Edomites lived at one time. This issue will also be dealt with later.

The exact conditions in the world at this time has also been the subject of some debate. Some have said that at the beginning of the week the Gog and Magog invasion of Israel will take place. Others have placed this just before the 70th week. They then speculate a short time of "peace and safety" at the beginning of this period. The theory has been advanced that the beast will first appear as a man of charisma and peaceful intentions. This is short lived for then "sudden destruction comes upon them" (I Thessalonians 5:3). Others have advanced the view that the "peace and safety" condition will only apply to Israel. They believe this condition will be present during the first half of the week when Israel has a covenant with other nations and this covenant will be enforced by the "prince that shall come" (Daniel 9:26), whom they believe will become the beast in the middle of the week. At that time sudden destruction comes upon them. According to this view the time of "great tribulation" (Matthew 24:21) will be at the middle of the week and will apply to the Jews and the saints only. Others apply two terms - tribulation and great tribulation - to the entire 70th week. They apply the term tribulation to the first and great tribulation to the second half. In 2nd Thessalonians 2:6 & 7 there is a discussion of the restraint of evil and the evil one. When the restraint and restraining One is removed then lawlessness and the lawless one of the tribulation period can manifest themselves. There is debate among commentators about the identity of the restrainer. Most believe the restrainer to be the Holy Spirit but some think the Archangel Michael. A few have said the Roman Empire but they may be associated with some view other than the pre-tribulation rapture view. There will be much discussion later on several of these ideas.

The subject matter of the Olivet discourse has been a matter of much discussion This discourse is found in Matthre 24 & 25, Mark 13 and two chapters in Luke (17 & 21) but at a different geographical location. Matthew's version is most often used. Some have said the opening verses (4-8) refer to the course of this present age, others seem to apply them to the last days of this age, while others apply them to the early part of the 70th week. There seems to be somewhat of a parallel between these verses and the first 8 verses of Revelation 6. it is universally agreed that Revelation 6 refers to the 70th week. The "gospel of the kingdom" (verse 14) is not being preached today. It seems very obvious to me that the teachings or events of these verses are not in sequential order. Just as the book of Revelation moves back and forth in time so do the verses of this chapter. Many questions can be raised concerning the interpretation of these verses and will be dealt with in a later chapter.

A key element in the pretribulation rapture discussion is the teaching concerning imminency Imminency is considered by some to be the cornerstone of the pretribulation view. Many New testament passages appear to teach imminency (I Cor. 1:7; 16:22; Phil. 3;20 4:5; I The. 1:10; Titus 2:13; Heb. 9:28; James 5:7-9; I Pet. 1:13; Jude 21; Rev. 3:11; 22:7, 12, 20). Of the verses mentioned seven of them appear not only to teach imminency but nearness of the Lord's coming.

> Phil. 4:5 "The Lord is at hand."
>
> James 5:8 "The coming of the Lord is at hand."
>
> James 5:9 "Behold, the Judge is standing at the door!"
>
> Rev. 3:11 "Behold, I come quickly!"
>
> Rev. 22:7 "Behold, I am coming quickly!"
>
> Rev. 22:12 "And behold, I am coming quickly..."
>
> Rev. 22:20 "Surely, I am coming quickly."

This creates a problem since over 19 centuries have passed since then. An attempt will be made to deal with this problem in a later chapter.

Another problem to be considered which relates to imminency is that of last days prophecy, and by that I mean prophecy relating to the last days of this present church age. There are many commentators who have applied various prophecies to this present age particularly with regard to the newly formed nation of Israel This would violate the principle of imminency for it required a fulfillment of prophecy before the rapture. But there are three definite areas of Scripture which give prophecies for the latter days of this present church age. These are: I Tim 4:1-5; 2 Tim. 3:1-9; 2 Pet. 3:3-6. In John 2:18 we read "it is the last hour" and we wonder how long can the last hour last? Some have said that the last days and the last hour are the entire church age. I believe this subject should have a complete reexamination.

Joel's prophecy has been the subject of various interpretations. There is uncertainty concerning the date when Joel was written. There is no Biblical or other record of this invasion of Israel by a horde of locusts such as described here. Some have given the text a double meaning; one literal and one pictorial. The pictorial view says an invading army (of men) is described here, probably referring to the invasion by Gog and Magog described in Ezekiel 38 and 39. On the day of Pentecost Peter quotes Joel 2:28-32. The 28th verse refers to the pouring out of the Spirit on all flesh. Some say this was the fulfillment of this prophecy; others say this was a sample of what the future fulfillment will be like. Another rapture view uses verse 31 as part of its Biblical foundation. Verse 31 says "The sun shall be turned into darkness, and the moon into blood, before the coming of the great and terrible day of the Lord." These cosmic disturbances parallel the events of the sixth seal in Revelation 6. The argument is then made that the day of the Lord is the day of the Lord's wrath, i.e. the trumpet and bowl judgments. Since the saints are not to be victims of God's wrath the assertion is made that the rapture should occur at the end of the sixth seal just before the outpouring of God's wrath in the following judgments. In chapter 3, verse 12 it says: "For there I will sit to judge all the surrounding nations." Some have equated this with the judgment of the nations in Matt. 25:31-46. Most, however, equate this with Armageddon. An examination of Joel will be considered in a later chapter.

CHAPTER 2

GOG AND MAGOG

In the "latter years" or "latter days", there will be an invasion of Israel by an alliance of nations, Gog of the land of Magog being the leader and most important one. This has been the subject of much discussion among prophecy teachers, particularly since the rise and subsequent fall of the Russian Empire, since Russia is considered to be the land of Magog by nearly all expositors. Their armies are said to come from the north parts but are also accompanied by nations from northern Africa as well as nations from Europe and also Persia (Iran). These are the principal players in this drama, but Ez. 38:9 says, concerning the invasion, "you and all your troops and many peoples with you." Evidently, there are people from other nations joining them. It is thought that the names Rosh, Meshech, and Tubal are thought to refer to Russia, Moscow, and Tobolsk. Others have associated some of these names with Turkey. Turkey is north of Israel but the words, "far north" (verse 15) some have taken to indicate a nation further to the north, hence the idea of Russia. There is, of course, a historical basis for all attempts to identify these nations.

The purpose of this chapter is to further attempt to identify these nations but also to challenge the accepted timing of this event. As stated in the previous chapter, there is almost universal agreement that this invasion will occur just prior to Daniel's 70th week or sometime during this period, probably early in the first half. Numerous attempts have been made to reconcile these ideas with the book of Revelation as well as the Olivet discourse (Matt. 24 and Mark 13). Some have attempted to associate this invasion with certain battles described in Dan. 11:40 and 44. The last ten verses in Dan. 11 (36 - 45) describe the conquests of the antichrist, whereas the invasion described in Ez. 38 and 39 is an unchallenged invasion of Israel where God alone defeats the enemy. In Rev. 6:1-8 and Matt. 24:6 - 8, we have a description of the conquests of the antichrist during what many believe to be the first half of Daniel's 70th week.. There is no mention or possibility of Ezekiel's invasion occurring during this time. Because of this some have thought the invasion took place just prior to Daniel's 70th week, while others have suggested Ezekiel's invasion took place at the very beginning of the 70th week and the antichrist's conquests will take place after Ezekiel's invasion but still within the 70th week time frame. It is this authors belief that this invasion from the north will not take place in this time period at all.

Let us digress for a moment. The big difference between millenarian and amillenarian views of interpretation is whether or not to interpret the prophetic Scriptures literally. Since we who are millenarians take the prophetic Scriptures literally, let us consider that idea now with respect to several statements in Ezekiel's prophecy. Every reader knows what kind of world we live in, how wars are fought, what nations are the wealthiest, and most know which nations are the enemies with certain others. Consider Ez. 38:4 "I will turn you around, put hooks into your jaws, and lead you out, with all your army, horses, and horsemen, all splendidly clothed, a great company, with bucklers and shields, all of them handling swords." Verse 5 also: Persia, Ethiopia, and Libya are with them, all of them with shield and helmet." Verse 15: 'Then you will come from your place out of the far north, you and many peoples with you, all of them riding on horses, a great company and a mighty army." Verse 21: "I will call for a sword against Gog throughout all My mountains, says the Lord God. Every man's sword will be against his brother." Ez. 39:3, "Then I will knock the bow out of your left hand, and cause the arrows to fall out of your right hand." Verse 9: "Then those who dwell in the cities of Israel will go out and set fire and burn the weapons, both the shields and bucklers, the bows and arrows, the javelins and spears; and they will make fires with them for seven years." In verse 20, we read of birds and beasts of the field being called to a sacrificial meal: "You shall be filled at My table with horse and riders, with mighty men and with all the men of war, says the Lord God." Surely, no one would try to fit this description in with today's military encounters. Since this battle has never occurred in the past and does not fit in today's world where shall we put it? Certainly not in the very near future.

The reason given for the invasion in Ez. 38:12 is "to take plunder and to take booty, to stretch out your hand against the waste places that are again inhabited, and against a people gathered from the nations, who have acquired livestock and goods who dwell in the midst of the land." In the next verse question is asked "Have you come to take plunder? Have you gathered your army to take booty, to carry away silver and gold, to take away livestock and goods, to take great plunder?" Envy seems to be the reason behind all of this. There is no mention of Jerusalem, the Temple Mount, the Dead Sea, the Islamic religion or any hint of antisemitism. It seems inconceivable that at this point in time and with the existing pressures on that tiny nation that this kind of wealth could accumulate. When it comes to wealth, what about the U.S., or Biblical Babylon of Revelation 18? Yet it is clearly stated here that Israel is an extremely wealthy and prosperous nation.

Another point to be made is the conditions under which Israel exists. Consider the following quotations which show the people of Israel to be living, not just prosperously as we have shown, but also peacefully, and appear to be in a right relationship with God.

Ez. 38:8 "they were brought out of the nations, and now all of them dwell safely."

38:11 " You will say, I will go up against a land of unwalled villages; I will go to a peaceful people, who dwell safely, all of them dwelling without walls, and having neither bars nor gates."

38:14 "My people Israel"

39:13 "the people of the land will be burying them, and they will gain renown for it on the day that I am glorified"

There are those who claim that Israel will be living peacefully in the first half of the 70th week because of an enforced treaty made by the Roman Prince of Daniel 9:27, but reread these quotes and see if that solution is satisfying. Also, that would eliminate the idea of this battle occurring before the 70th week. Some point to Ez. 39:22 as proof that this is the time of Israel's conversion. This cannot be true. Zechariah 13:8 & 9 tells us that 2/3 of the nation will be cut off and die during the last half of the 70th week and the third part will be refined and tested, and finally will be called His people. Besides this the 12th chapter of Zechariah (verse 10 - 14) tell us quite vividly of the conversion of Israel when "they will look on Me whom they have pierced; they will mourn for Him as one mourns for his only son, and grieve for Him as one grieves for a firstborn." In the context of the first 9 verses of Chapter 12 this appears to happen at the end of the 70th week. The first verse of the next chapter (13) makes it conclusive that this is the time of Israel's conversion.

"In that day a fountain shall be opened for the house of David and for the inhabitants of Jerusalem, for sin and for uncleanness."

Reminds one of that old hymn:

There is a fountain filled with blood

Drawn from Immanuel's veins,

And sinners plunged beneath that flood

Lose all their guilty stains.

Let us consider the distances involved for the invaders coming to Israel. From Moscow to the "mountains of Israel" would be somewhere in the neighborhood of 2,000 miles. That is a pretty good trek on horseback for, perhaps, millions of horsemen prepared for battle. Let's not forget either that these men are expecting to carry back much booty with them. The distance from Teheran to the same area would be about 800 miles, still a good trek, but well within the realm of possibility. It seems that Turkey and certain North African nations are closest and could easily invade Israel. In a reference Bible I have, the notes on Ezekiel 38 inform me that this prophecy refers to Russia and other allied nations. In the back of this same Bible, a map of the Near East at about the 8th century BC gives the names Meshech, Tubal , Gomer, and Togarmah in what is present day Turkey. Another source of information indicates that Rosh was located along the Tigris River, probably in Persia (Iran). It also says that Magog was probably in the Western part of present day Turkey. It may be that in later centuries descendants of these people moved further north, but in Ezekiel's day, the names given here are not far removed from Israel. It makes much more sense to believe that Turkey, certain North African nations and Iran could be the invaders. If the nation of Israel was extended further toward the east (as it will be in the millennium) Iran could be its neighbor. If one looked at a map of the near east and imagined an enlarged Israel (reaching to the Euphrates, Gen. 16:18) these nations would almost surround Israel.

There are two other views concerning the timing of this event. One view places this invasion in the millennium, the other at the end of the period. Since the kingdom age is described as an age of peace, health, longevity, etc., and the Devil is bound for 1,000 years, it seems extremely unlikely that during this period such an event as this would occur. On the other hand, we are told in Rev. 20:7 - 10 that there will be an invasion of Israel by Gog and Magog at the end of the 1,000 year period. It has been asserted that there are certain differences in the two accounts. Ezekiel's version names certain nations or peoples but the book of Revelation says that Satan will "go out to deceive the nations which are in the four quarters of the earth." It should be remembered that Ezekiel says that in addition to the invading troops there will be "many peoples with you." Ezekiel's version describes several means used to destroy the invaders, but Revelation says that fire will come down from God out of heaven and devour them. Although Ezekiel's version mentions different means to destroy the invaders yet we find destruction by fire mentioned twice and brimstone once. The Revelation version appears to be a synopsis of the Ezekiel version with the intent of showing the timing of this event. Ezekiel's version says that God will put hooks into their jaws and bring them forth, while the book of Re velation says Satan will gather them together to battle, but God neither tempts or causes man to sin.

The book of Revelation contains some new prophetic material, but its purpose seems to be to put all prophetic material into one complete, coherent picture. According to the most commonly held view the Ezekiel invasion, with all its details, does not appear anywhere in the book of Revelation. At the same time the invasion of Rev. 20:7 - 10 does not appear anywhere else in the bible even though the names (Gog and Magog) are the same as used by Ezekiel.

It has been asserted by some that the Ezekiel invasion of chapters 38 and 39 is sandwiched between the return of the Jews to the land prior to this in chapters 36 and 37, and a lengthy, detailed, description of the millennial temple, worship, and other conditions in the land of Israel during that kingdom age. Two things must be said about this. First, the return of Israel as described here is at the end of the 70th week, not prior to it. A preliminary return and rebuilding of the temple is implied in places such as Dan. 9:27 and II Thes. 2:4. There have always been Jewish people in the land.

Second, even a casual reading of Ez. 35:25 - 38 and Ez. 37:22-28 will reveal that the nation of Israel is in the kingdom age at this time.

The effect of God's victory over the invaders upon the Gentile nations is stated in Ez. 38:23 and Ex. 39:7 and possibly 39:13 & 21. The theme is, the nations shall know that He is the Lord. If this invasion took place in the early part of the 70th week (or before) this statement could not be true. Consider the events that will take place during the remainder of the 70th week. This is the time when many (probably most) will worship the devil, the beast, and his image. See Rev. 13:3, 4, 7, 8, and 15. It is the time of the judgments of God being poured out on a rebellious, unbelieving world, climaxing in the battle of Armageddon, which is then followed by the judgment of the remaining nations (Matt.25:31 - 46). It appears to be the exact opposite of what we would expect from the statements in Ezekiel.

In Ez. 38:8 and 16, we find the words "latter years" and "latter days." The following prophetic passages in Ezekiel speak of end time events:

Ez. 11:17 - 20

Ez. 16:60 - 63

Ez. 20:33 - 44

Ez. 36, 37, 40 - 48

In not one of these passages do we find a reference to latter years or latter days. If the most popular view is correct then all these passages would be speaking of events taking place after all these other prophecies have been fulfilled. Hence, it would not be proper to have the terms latter years and latter days applied here and not in those passages.

Some times when writing, one might have other thoughts, such is the case here. After finishing this chapter and continuing on; I became aware of a view held by a small group of prophecy teachers; i.e. the battle of Gog and Magog is either the same as the battle of Armageddon or, at least, part of a series of the end time, as described in Ezekiel 38 & 39. Revelation tells of a world almost totally destroyed by the trumpet and bowl judgments, or persecutions of Israel, and part of the Jewish remnant having fled into the wilderness, and Jerusalem's Jews being deported after the invasion of that city. Ezekiel, on the other hand, tells of a people in Israel being very prosperous and living at peace, as well as other Gentile nations verbally challenging the invaders. These conditions seem to be exact opposites. More will be said about Armageddon in the next chapter.

CHAPTER 3

ARMAGEDDON - WHY?

T he climax of this age will be the battle of Armageddon and three entities will be involved - God, Satan and his hosts, and unregenerate mankind. The goal of all three will be the same, to get armies of men to come to battle against Israel. It will be quite similar to the battle of Gog and Magog in the previous chapter, the difference being the goal of the invading armies. In the battle of Gog and Magog, the goal was to take spoil; in the battle of Armageddon the goal will be to annihilate Israel.

In the days of Noah, God destroyed all the inhabitants of the world except for eight people. In the case of Sodom and Gomorrah, there were not ten righteous people in those cities so God caused Lot's family to leave before destroying everyone else. In both cases, the reason was the same; the people turned a deaf ear to the message God had for them. Their lives were lived in defiance of Him. His patience ran out, His holiness was vindicated, his wrath and power were displayed. So it shall be at the end of this age. After incredible judgments were poured out on mankind their reactions were as follows:

Revelation 9:20 - 21 "But the rest of mankind, who were not killed by these plagues, did not repent of the works of their hands, that they should not worship demons, and idols of gold, silver, brass, stone, and wood, which can neither see nor hear nor walk; and did not repent of their murders or their sorceries, or their sexual immorality or their thefts."

Revelation 16:11 "And they blasphemed the God of heaven because of their pains and their sores, and did not repent of their deeds."

The fact is plain that God Himself is causing men to come down to His land and His people of war.

Joel 3:2 "I will also gather all nations, and bring them down to the Valley of Jehoshaphat; and I will enter into judgment with them there."

Joel 3:9- 12 "Proclaim this among the nations: prepare for war! Wake up the mighty men, let all the men of war draw near, let them come up. Beat your plowshares into swords and your pruning hooks into spears; let the weak say, I am strong, assemble and come, all you nations, gather together all around, cause Your mighty ones to go down there, O Lord. Let the nations be wakened, and come up to the Valley of Jehoshaphat; for there I will sit to judge all the surrounding nations."

This reminds us of the preceding chapter concerning the invasion of Gog and Magog where we read:

Ez. 38:4 "I will turn you around, put hooks into your jaws, and lead you out, with all your army."

The sovereignty of God must always be included in any consideration of end time events. There is an interesting account in I Kings 22 of the Lord using a lying spirit to deceive King Ahab that he might go to battle and be slain; the heavenly scene records the following:

> I Kings 22:20-23 "And the Lord said, who will persuade Ahab to go up, that he may fall at Ramoth Gilead? So one spoke in this manner, and another spoke in that manner. Then a spirit came forward and stood before the Lord, and said, I will persuade him. The Lord said to him, In what way? So he said, I will go out and be a lying spirit in the mouth of all his prophets. And He said, You shall persuade him, also prevail. Go out and do so. Now therefore, look! The Lord has put a lying spirit in the mouth of all these prophets of yours, and the Lord has declared disaster against you."

In Revelation 16 we read of the Lord preparing the way for the kings and their armies to come to battle at the end time.

> Rev. 16:12 "Then the sixth angel poured out his bowl in the great river Euphrates, and its water was dried up, so that the way of the kings from the east might be prepared."

But notice what follows:

> Rev. 16:13, 14 &16 "And I saw three unclean spirits like frogs, coming out of the mouth of the dragon, out of the mouth of the beast, out of the mouth of the false prophet, for they are spirits of demons, performing signs, which go out to the kings of the earth and of the whole world, to gather them to the battle of that

great day of God Almighty. And they gathered them together to the place called in Hebrew, Armageddon."

It makes one wonder what takes place in the minds of Satan and his demons. The demons appear to know about their coming fate (Matt. 8:29). Satan also seems to be very much aware of his fate (Rev. 12:12). In the verse mentioned it speaks of the devil having great wrath even though he knows his time is short. Five verses later in verse 17 mention is made of the dragon (Satan) being enraged with the woman (Israel) and going off to make war with the rest of her offspring. At the end of the millennium after 1,000 years of imprisonment, Satan is loosed for a short time, and immediately he gathers nations to go to war against Israel, even though he knows his eternal doom is quickly coming. James 2:19 mentions that demons tremble because of their knowledge of God. It seems that in the mind of the devil and his demons fear and wrath coexists, and this right down to the very end. I Cor. 10:20 says the Gentiles sacrifice to demons and Rev. 13:4 tells us that in that future day the world will worship the devil. Is it possible that in the future day satanic forces gathering the nations for Armageddon could possibly think that they could win, or will they just take delight in the slaughter of millions of Gentiles, most of whom worshiped the devil. Similarly at the end of the millennium the devil will attempt the impossible, having just been loosed after 1,000 years imprisonment, making another futile attempt to destroy Israel. It all seems so irrational. There are many brilliant scientists who embrace a totally ridiculous theory of evolution. Could satanic forces be as foolish having been in the presence of God Himself, to think they could thwart the purposes of God? Unlikely; I think that they, unlike humans, though they know fear, cannot be paralyzed by it, and, therefore, will vent their wrath to the very last second.

What about the Gentile nations, why will they climax their existence at Armageddon? It seems to be a combination of wrath and hope- a futile hope. To answer this question we must trace the events of Revelation. The author assumes at this point that the average reader of this book has some knowledge of the book of Revelation. If this is not so, it is suggested that the reader now read through, and familiarize himself, herself, with its contents. Chapter 6 through 19 are concerned with the judgments of God and climax at Armageddon. There are 21 judgments, seven seals, are in a sense, man made. They are all calamities associated with war and lawlessness. At that point in time man will have himself to blame, but thereafter everything changes. God intervenes to prevent man from destroying himself, and to demonstrate His power and wrath, while still offering salvation. The following list of judgment will enable the reader to appreciate the magnitude of these judgments.

Great earthquake.

Sun become black as sackcloth of hair.

Moon became like blood.

Stars fall to earth.

Sky recedes as a scroll. (Though part of the sixth seal this may come later.)

Every mountain and island moved out of its place.

Noises, thunderings, lightnings, and an earthquake.

Hail, fire, and blood thrown to the earth.

End of the seal judgments.

A third of the trees burned up.

All green grass burned up.

A mountain burning with fire thrown into the sea.

A third of the sea became blood.

A third of living creatures in the sea died.

A third of the ships were destroyed.

A star burning like a torch fell from heaven.

It turned one third of fresh water to wormwood.

A third of sun, moon, and stars darkened - a third of the day and the night darkened.

Demonic creatures torment men for five months - like the sting of a scorpion.

Other creatures slay one third of mankind with fire, smoke and brimstone.

Lightning, noises, thunderings, an earthquake, and great hail.

That list took us to the end of the trumpet judgments, the bowl judgments are yet to come. The bowl judgments are even more severe. At this point, we must consider something else that has been happening. There are two witnesses (possibly Moses and Elijah) who have been prophesying for 1,260 days (half of that 70th week), apparently in the area of Jerusalem. When their enemies attempt to destroy them fire proceeds from their mouth, and destroys their enemies. Rev. 12:6 says "These have power to shut heaven, so that no rain falls in the days of their prophecy, and they have power over waters to turn them to blood, and to strike the earth with all plagues, as often as they desire." It is easy to see that the inhabitants of the earth will blame the judgments on these two witnesses. At the end of their testimony the beast and his forces will be enabled to kill them. The nations by the way of TV will be able to see their bodies lying in the streets of Jerusalem for 3 1/2 days. They will have a Christmas type celebration for "These two prophets tormented those who dwell on the earth" (Rev. 11:10)/ after 3 1/2 days they are resurrected and "ascended to heaven in a cloud, and their enemies saw them" Rev. 11:12). It is at this point the world has a feeling of utter hopelessness. Take notice of the end of Rev 11:13

where it says "and the rest were afraid and gave glory to the God of heaven." See how different that is from Rev. 16: 9 & 21 where men are unrepentant after judgment. I believe this is the time Zech. 12:10 to 13:1 is fulfilled - the time of Israel's conversion- they have become convinced of the resurrection of Christ after seeing this resurrection experience.

Following this come the bowl judgments:

> Foul and loathsome sore on men who had the mark of the beast.

> Entire sea became blood.

> Every creature in the sea died.

> All fresh water became blood.

> Sun scorched men.

> Darkness and pain.

> Euphrates dried up, three unclean spirits go out to deceive men - preparation for Armageddon.

> Seventh bowl - great earthquake destroying the cities of the earth, mountains and islands disappear, great hailstones fall on men - probably the same time as Armageddon.

> The earth has become uninhabitable.

I believe we must read between the lines. When the two witnesses were slain judgment was temporarily suspended (3 1/2 days). After their resurrection, judgments resumed. (I think there is good Biblical evidence the bowl judgments will last 30 days.) After the first five bowl judgments, three deceiving unclean spirits working miracles have a message for the nations. Some Jews were in Jerusalem and others have returned who were under God's protection for 1,260 days. Remember when the two witnesses were slain and the judgments stopped and they had a celebration - well, the message is - Jerusalem is the problem! If they can destroy the temple, the entire city, every Jew in the land and completely devastate the land, their problems will be over. Thus, every able-bodied, unregenerate man who has rejected the kingdom message will have another message which will send him to his doom. Readers may want to read the first nine verses of Zechariah 12 for more details on this. The divine viewpoint is different - see Joel 3:2.

CHAPTER 4

Petra

P etra has been a place of interest and speculation to many Bible prophecy teachers. South of the Dead Sea it was prominent in Old Testament history as the capital of the Edomites, descendants of Esau. A natural fortification, it has an entrance at one end through a narrow pass with overhanging cliffs about a mile long. Inside the Edomites built the rose red city of Petra carving rooms out of solid rock. Before the days of modern warfare it was considered a safe place to be. Some time before World War II some recognition of Petra as the place where Israel would flee during the tribulation period began to take place. The idea has become increasingly popular since then, being embraced by many prophecy teachers.

In Matt. 24:15 & 16 the Jews living in Judea are instructed to flee to the mountains when they see the "abomination of desolation" spoken of by Daniel the prophet standing in the holy place. See also Mark 13:14; Revelation 12 gives us more details of this flight to safety. It speaks of the dragon or serpent (the devil) attempting to persecute the woman (Israel).

> Rev 12:14 "But the woman was given two wings of a great eagle, that she might fly into the wilderness to her place, where she is nourished for a time and times and half a time (3 1/2 years) from the presence of the serpent."

There is no question then, about the fact that many Jews will flee to some place in the mountainous or wilderness area in the middle of the 70th week to escape the persecution by the antichrist. According to Zech. 13:18 two thirds of the people in all the land shall be cut off and die. Where to go, and why, must not be viewed from a purely human view point; the supernatural hand of God must be seen in all this. Consider again, Rev 12:14 "But the woman was given two wings of a great eagle, that she might fly into the wilderness to her place, where she is nourished for a time and times and half a time." When Israel wandered in the wilderness for forty years God took care of them; it appears this will happen again, this time for 3 1/2 years.

There will necessarily be a place provided for some of those in Israel to be protected and preserved (note that this does not include all in Israel). We have two choices here; either God will take care of His people in a place already in existence (such as Petra), or He will at this particular time provide a special place for them. I will attempt to present a view which may be met with much resistance. Consider the following verses which are familiar to many.

Zech. 14:4 & 5 "And in that day His feet will stand on the Mount of Olives, which faces Jerusalem on the east. And the Mount of Olives shall be split in two, from east to west, making a very large valley; half of the mountain shall move toward the north, and half of it toward the south. Then you shall flee through My mountain valley, for the mountain valley, shall reach to Azal, yes, you shall flee as you fled from the earthquake in the days of Uzziah king of Judah. Thus the Lord my God will come, and all the saints with You (or Him)."

Everyday prophecy teacher I have ever heard has placed this event at the end of the tribulation period. The reason for this is the end of this verse - "thus the Lord my God will come, and all the saints with You (or Him)." The assumption is "Thus the Lord my

God will come" = "Immediately the Lord my God will come." When we compare portions of prophetic Scripture with other portions (particularly with the book of Revelation) we often find there are pieces (events) missing from the puzzle which make the whole scenario. One example would be Matthew 24 where the narrative goes directly from the sixth seal of Revelation 6 to Armageddon in Revelation 19. the prophet Joel does the same thing. None of the prophetic Scriptures appear to contain any references to the trumpet and bowl judgments found in the book of Revelation (there may be some slight hint of them in chapter 24 and 26 of the book of Isaiah, and Matt. 24:21 "Great Tribulation.")

> Zech 14:1 & 2 "Behold the day of the Lord is coming, and your spoil will be divided in your midst, for I will father all the nations to battle against Jerusalem, the city shall be taken, the houses rifled, and the women ravished, half the city shall go into captivity, but the remnant of the people shall not be cut off from the city."

How can anyone familiar with prophecy say that these things will take place at the time of Armageddon? This is the time when the militarily successful forces of the antichrist invade Jerusalem; take everything they want, take advantage of the women, and deport half of the people. Let's compare it with the previous chapter.

> Zecharaiah 13:8- 9 "and it shall come to pass in all the land, says the Lord, that two thirds in it shall be cut off and die, but one third shall be left in it; I will bring the one third through the fire, will refine them as silver is refined, and test them as gold is tested......"

Certainly this speaks of that 3 1/2 year period when the Gentiles "tread the holy city under for forty-two months" (Rev. 11:2). The time when Jerusalem is invaded, people are deported and slain in the same time when the antichrist will "plant the tents of his palace between the seas and the glorious holy mountain (Dan.12:45), and "sits as God in the temple of God, showing himself that he is God (II Thes. 2:4). This is the time when they are warned to flee to the mountains. Verse 5 of chapter 14 tells them to flee through His mountain valley. Zech.14:2 says half of the city shall go into captivity, and Zech. 1:8 says in all the land two thirds shall be cut off; certainly they are speaking of the same time and event. If this is not the case what is the purpose of splitting the Mount of Olives? Zechariah tells us in verses 4 & 5 of chapter 14 just quoted. The purpose is to create a great valley in the mountains for the people to flee into, evidently for their own preservation, for this is the time when people are being deported from Jerusalem. Note that they are twice told to flee through this valley in the mountains, and the urgency of the situation is made even more clear for they are told to flee as they fled before the earthquake in the days of Uzziah.

Chapter 12 speaks very clearly about the end time invasion (Armageddon) of Jerusalem and Judea. A few quotes for comparison.

> Zech. 12:2 "Behold, I will make Jerusalem a cup of drunkenness (trembling" - AV) to all the surrounding peoples, when they lay siege against Judea and Jerusalem. "(Note the word "siege")

> Zech. 12:3 "And it shall happen in that day that I will make Jerusalem a very heave stone for all peoples, all who would heavy it away will surely be cut in pieces, though all nations of the earth are gathered against it." (The city is not captured)

> Zech 12:4 "In that day, says the Lord, I will strike every horse with confusion, and its rider with madness …."

> Zech 12:6 "In that day I will make the governors of Judah like a fire pan in the woodpile, and like a fiery torch in the sheaves; they shall devour all the surrounding people on the right hand and on the left ……"

Zech 12:8 "In that day the Lord will defend the inhabitants of Jerusalem; the one who is feeble among them in that day shall be like David, and the house of David shall be like God, like the Angel of the Lord before them." (No one fleeing at this time.)

Zech. 12:9 "It shall be in that day that I will seek to destroy all the nations that come against Jerusalem.

One cannot help but see a striking contrast here.

Probably the primary reason why the splitting of the Mount of Olives is thought to be at the end of the tribulation period is because of the last part of Zech. 14:6 "….Thus the Lord my God will come and all the saints with You (or Him). "We must remember this is Zechariah, not Daniel or Revelation; all the parts of the prophetic picture are not contained in this portion. Where, in all of Scripture, do we find the trumpet and bowl judgments? In the last three chapters of Zechariah there is an obvious moving back and forth in time in the prophetic picture, particularly in chapter 14. compare in chapter 14:8 - 11 with the following verses 12- 15.

A word of criticism and exhortation. Many times I heard people speak of a crack or fault line in the region of the Mount of Olives. Is He God or isn't He? Those who say such things may be well meaning, but I believe there is no reason to find such "evidences" to prove His word. God's word is powerful and there are many other ways to prove its trustworthiness

Finally, one of the purposes of the book of Revelation is to put the pieces of the prophetic puzzle together, and if this fleeing through the mountain valley is not the same as the fleeing of the woman (Israel) into the wilderness in Revelation 12 then we have no clue as to where this event fits into the picture, at least, not from the book of Revelation.

CHAPTER 5

PEACE AND SAFETY

The words "peace and safety" or probably better, "peace and security" are found in I Thes. 5:3. "For when they say, peace and safety then sudden destruction will come upon them, as labor pains upon a pregnant woman. And they shall not escape." The context is "the day of the Lord" in verse 2. thus it should be concluded that the day of the Lord (which comes as a thief in the night - verse 2) will come suddenly and unexpectedly. The view that one has of the day of the Lord will determine when in the prophetic scenario this event will take place. Some insist this is the battle of Gog and Magog which they believe occurs either just before, or just inside the 70th week. Others believe it starts with the first seal of Rev. 6 which pictures a man riding on a white horse going forth conquering and to conquer. Still others place this at a later seal (perhaps the second). They say this because the first riders are said to have a bow, but no arrows are mentioned, thus making him a peaceful, charismatic leader. They reinforce this view by referring to Dan. 11:24 which mentions a man entering peaceably into the richest places of the province before showing his real intentions. They apply this prophecy to the antichrist.

Still other believe the day of the Lord begins with, or just after, the sixth seal, insisting that the day of the Lord means the day of the Lord's wrath. They then point out that the previous seals are man's doing's or man's wrath, and what follows are judgments from God. According to this view by the fifth seal, which in Revelation emphasizes martyrdom, is a time of peace and security for the rest of the world. Therefore, at the end of this period the sixth seal puts an end to their peace and safety when cosmic disturbances bring calamity to earth's inhabitants. I do not agree.

In the book of Zephaniah, which is a book that warns Israel and also surrounding nations of a coming judgment, this judgment being primarily the result of Babylonian invasions, though there appear to be some references to end time events, carry the following references to the day of the Lord.

> Zeph. 1:7 "day of the Lord."
>
> Zeph. 1:8 "day of the Lord's sacrifice."
>
> Zeph 1:14 "great day of the Lord."
>
> Zeph. 1:18 "day of the Lord's wrath."
>
> Zeph. 2:2 "day of the Lord's anger."

Though there are some end time references, these verses all appear to point to the coming invasions by the Babylonians. Though the day of the Lord may refer to different things in different places it seems obvious here that it can refer to wars and their associated difficulties. Though men don't seem to want to recognize it, the Bible teaches that war often is either God's instrument for testing, or punishment for sin. The innocent perish with the guilty. It should be pointed out here that the sixth seal, not the seventh, or the trumpet judgments, is the start of the direct hand of God in judgment (if we consider the wars and persecutions to be indirect). "The great day of His wrath has come" Rev. 6:17.

The issue of Gog and Magog has been dealt with in a previous chapter and will not be dealt with again. This leaves us with either the first or second seal as the time when peace and security are done away with. We will deal with the second seal first (I don't see how they can make it the third or fourth seal). as stated previously, there is a commonly held view that the rider on the white horse, though known to be the antichrist, is introduced here as a charismatic, peaceful leader coming onto the world stage. The argument is made that he has a bow and no arrows. Does this make sense? There are other verses in the Bible that mention a bow without arrows, but the implication is certainly there. This man on the white horse (sign of victory) is seen with a crown given to him and he "went out conquering and to conquer" with an unloaded gun. Sorry, I just can't see it that way. Previously, we mentioned a verse in Daniel 11 used to give support to this idea. The verse reads as follows:

> Dan. 11:24 "He shall enter peaceably, even into the richest places of the province; ....and he shall devise his plans against the strongholds........."

Daniel 11 deals with the Grecian Empire and its history after the death of Alexander the Great. His kingdom was divided among four generals according to the four points of the compass. At verse five, it deals with the kings of the South and North. These were the ones who overran and controlled Israel during part of the intertestamental period. In verse 21 we read the rise of a "vile person", Antiochus Epiphanes. The narrative concerns him at least to verse 32; then a transition to the end time occurs up to verse 35. Verse 36 then begins to deal with a "willful king" down to the end of the chapter. Most commentators of the pretribulational view agree with this. Verse 24 then, has to do with Antichus Epiphanes, not the antichrist. The problem here seems to be an addiction to typology. Typology is part of the Scripture but the application of it can be taken to extremes. Why apply this small portion of the narrative to the antichrist and not the rest of it? Historical records verify the events of this account. Ask any orthodox Jew about

Hanukkah and he will be able to verify the last few verses of this portion about Antiochus.

I believe the best scenarios is that peace and security vanish with the appearance of Antichrist. In the 11th chapter of Daniel (verse 36-45) with the appearance and warmonger. In Rev. 6:1, he first appears on a white horse going forth "conquering and to conquer." Revelation 17 seems to be telling us that the ten kings of the revived Roman Empire give their authority to the beast for the express purpose of destroying the harlot. Consider the following verses:

> Rev. 17:13 "These are of one mind, and they will give their power and authority to the beast."

> Rev. 17:16 & 17 "and the ten horns which you saw on the beast, these will hate the harlot, make her desolate and naked, eat her flesh and burn her with fire. For God has put into their heart to fulfill His purpose, to be of one mind, and to give their kingdom to the beast, until the words of God are fulfilled."

Destruction of the harlot seems to be his (their) first destructive art, the very reason for the formation of their alliance. The sudden rise to power of the beast is the apparent cause for the removal of peace and security from this world.

Our key verse, I Thes. 5:3 implies a future time (certainly not now - November 2018) when men, living apart from God, will have found a way to eliminate the threat of war (peace), and terrorism (security). There are two parts to this. Victory over Islamic terrorism will provide the security, but what about peace? I believe we are about to enter another period of cold war, and when this threat is finally overcome, then this prophecy can be fulfilled. I will deal more with this in Chapter 7 which will cover the four beasts of Daniel 7. The fact that men will take credit to themselves for achieving peace and security is the reason for what follows: "then sudden destruction will come upon them."

I believe after much meditation on this, that this verse does not refer to the destruction of Babylon by the beast and the kings, but rather to the "Day of the Lord" (previous verse) which is the beginning of the 3 1/2 years reign of the Beast which is the "Great Tribulation."

CHAPTER 6

RESTRAINING - RESTRAINER

II Thes. 2:6 & 7 "And now you know what is restraining, that he may be revealed in his own time. For the mystery of lawlessness is already at work; only He who now restrains will do so until He is taken out of the way."

These are the two verses we will be dealing with, and there have been several explanations offered for the two expressions, "what is restraining," and "He who now restrains." One explanation offered (probably the most popular) is that the One who restrains is the same One Who is restraining - the Holy Spirit. Since both neuter gender and masculine gender are used of the Holy Spirit in Scripture this explains the double usage here. According to this view the Holy Spirit is preventing the beast from appearing until his set time. The mystery of lawlessness which we can see already at work in our world, our society, is likewise being held back until "He is taken out the way." The expression "taken out of the way (not away) is generally associated with the removal of the church at the rapture. After this time we are told "lawlessness will abound"

Matt. 24:12, as one of the conditions of that future tribulation period. This view coincides the removal of the church with the removal of the restraining work of the Holy Spirit on society in general. Another view is that "Michael the Archangel shall stand up (they say stand up should stand aside), the great prince who stands watch over the sons of your people; and there shall be a time of trouble, such as never was since there was a nation......" (Dan 12:) The idea is that Michael is restraining evil, and when he stands aside evil will be unrestrained. But in Dan. 11:1 the same word is used of an angel standing up to confirm and strengthen another. The word is also used a second time in Dan. 12:1 :"the great prince who stands watch over the sons of your people." Still another view is the government of the old Roman Empire (at the time of Paul's writing) is the restraining influence on evil society. This idea belongs to an entirely different prophetic viewpoint than the one we are considering.

Verse three in our chapter says the day of the Lord will not come unless the falling away comes first. The Greek word apostasia translated falling away should be (or could be) translated departure some have said. This departure they consider to be the rapture, thus reinforcing their view that the restraining influence of the church will be removed at that time. It is interesting to note that this early church, which had very little teaching time under the apostle Paul, knew something we don't seem to know today, or, at least, is the subject of debate, Verse 6 says "And now you know what is restraining ......" I believe the restraining influence on world wide evil would have to be the work of the Holy Spirit. Who else, or what else, could possibly do this effectively? From observation I believe the church (salt of the earth, light of the world) is a restraint on evil. Politically, have we not seen the difference that moral leadership makes? Unquestionably, the spreading of the Gospel and teaching of the Scriptures is the number one factor in controlling evil. Men have been given a conscience by God but sometimes their conscience becomes "seared with a hot iron" (I Tim. 4:2).

There is a second issue here, i.e. the restraining of the evil one - the antichrist. Here we have the problem of the gender being neuter. I believe there is a better solution than to say the Holy Spirit is referred to in this way. The gender is neuter because it is not a person, or persons, being referred to here; rather, it is a "thing." I would like to raise a question for my reader; what restrains the devil during the millennium? The answer is found in the 20th chapter of Revelation.

> Rev. 20:1 - 3 "Then I saw an angel coming down from heaven, having key to the bottomless pit and a great chain in his hand. He laid hold of the dragon, that serpent of old, who is the Devil and Satan, and bound him for a thousand years, and he cast him into the bottomless put, and shut him up, and set a seal on him, so that he should deceive the nations no more till the thousand years were finished. But after these things he must be released for a little while."

A second question is this; where does the beast come from? Again, let us go to the book of Revelation, the 11th chapter which deals with the two witnesses who testify for 3 1/2 years.

> Rev. 11:7 "Now when they finish their testimony the beast that ascends out of the bottomless pit will make war against them, overcome them, and kill them."

A third question; is he there now? We will refer to Paul's discussion of him in his second epistle to the Thessalonians.

> II Thes. 2:6 "And now you know what is restraining, that he may be revealed in his own time."

Question number four; when did he go there? We don't know the exact time but we are told it was before John's day. Let's look at some end time passages in Revelation 17 for a little better picture.

> Rev. 17:8 "The beast that you saw was, and is not, and will ascend out of the bottomless pit and go to perdition. And those who dwell on the earth will marvel, whose names are not written in the Book of Life from the foundation of the world, when they see the beast that was, and is not, and yet is."

> Rev. 17:11 "And the beast that was, and is not, is himself also the eighth, and is of the seven, and is going to perdition."

This must not be confused with the "mortal wound" of Revelation 13; we will deal with that later. We cannot know about the spirit world except by revelation, but it is apparent spirits can be imprisoned (I Peter 3:19). It seems logical to conclude from the preceding verses that a person (a "king"Rev. 17:10) was consigned to the bottomless pit some time before John's day. He will return and indwell another body at the end time. Consider:

> Rev. 17:10 & 11 "There are also seven king. Five have fallen, one is, and the other has not yet come. And when he comes, he must continue a short time. And the beast that was, and is not, is himself also an eighth, and is of the seven, and is going to perdition."

This may seem like a radical departure from what is normally taught, but I encourage the reader to take the Scriptures literally and meditate on these verses.

Daniel Chapter 7

The seventh chapter of Daniel tells of Daniel's dream of four beats, which are four successive empires. The descriptions of the beats tell us much about the empires and their leaders. The most widely accepted interpretation of this chapter is that these empires are the same as the ones described in Daniel 2. Those empires are the Babylonian, Persian, Grecian, and Roman. These great empires of the past are pictured as an image (in King Nebuchadnezzar's dream), this image made of four different metals, gold, silver bronze, and iron going from top to bottom. Though we speak of the fall of the Roman Empire it appears from this image that this empire, though in disarray, is still with us (iron mixed with clay) because at the time of Christ's second coming the feet of this image are pictured as being smashed by a "smiting stone" which is Christ. There appears to be an effort under way to restore this empire today. Interestingly, not only the Roman Empire but also the other three empires are said to be smashed at the return of Christ. The assertion has been made that the image picture of the empires is the way man sees them, whereas the beasts of Daniel 7 picture them as God sees them. There is another view, however, which I favor and shall present my case now.

First, I shall present the reasons given for the most popular view. The description of the first beast is as follows:

> Dan. 7:4 "The first was like a lion, and had eagle's wings. I watched till its wings were plucked off; and it was lifted up from the earth and made to stand on two feet like a man, and a man's heart was given to it."

Sculpture of winged lions have been found in Babylon. The plucking of wings are supposed to represent the humbling of Nebuchadnezzar (Dan. 4), and the man's heart being given to it represents his apparent conversion.

The second beast is described in the next verse.

> Daniel 7:5 "And suddenly another beast, a second, like a bear. It was raised up on one side, and had three ribs in its mouth between its teeth. And they said thus to it; arise, devour much flesh."

Bears had been associated in ancient times with Persia. The empire was really made up of two groups, the Medes and Persians. It was just the Medes when it was raised up on one side, but when the Persians came in then it was told to "arise, devour much flesh."

The third beast is described next.

> Dan. 7:6 "After this I looked, and there was another, like a leopard, which had on its back four wings of a bird. The beast also had four heads, and dominion was given to it."

The swiftness of the leopard pictured the swift conquests of Greece under the leadership of Alexander the Great. When Alexander died, the kingdom was divided amount his four generals which are pictured by the four heads.

The final beast is now described.

> Dan. 7:7 "After this I saw in the night visions, and behold, a fourth beast, dreadful and terrible, exceedingly strong. It had huge iron teeth; it was devouring, breaking in pieces, and trampling the residue with its feet. It was different from all the beasts that were before it, it had ten horns."

This, of course, pictures Rome with its iron rule. The ten horns correspond obviously to the ten toes of the image of chapter 2, which, we are told, represent ten kings at the end time.

The other view is that the first three beasts represent three empires which come into existence during the time when the Roman Empire is in disarray. The fourth beast must necessarily be the Roman Empire, with the ten horns representing the ten kings of the final stage. This is the view I will attempt to establish.

The first beast is said to be Great Britain. The British lion is a term most of us are most familiar with; the eagle's wings would certainly be speaking of the United States. It's obvious what plucking of the eagle's wings represents. It is worth noting that although the third beast is a winged leopard this beast is specifically one that has "eagles" wings. If the lion refers to Babylon then a coherent interpretation must equate the lion with Nebuchadnezzar rather than with the empire of Babylon itself. Nebuchadnezzar had his wings plucked, he was given the heart of a man after his experience of seven years of insanity. Then apparently had some sort of conversion experience. With this kind of interpretation the eagles wings would be his pride. We must remember that the Babylonian Empire did not terminate with its leader having the "heart of a man" for King Belshazzar was perhaps worse than Nebuchadnezzar was in his earlier days. Daniel's vision occurred in the first year of Belshazzar's reign which was many years after the death of Nebuchadnezzar. If Nebuchadnezzar was the object of this vision then one-fourth of the vision would be history and three fourths would be prophecy. If we consider the lion to be the British Empire, then the beast being changed into the likeness of a man by standing on two feet and a man's heart being given to it represents a dramatic change in the British Empire. The modern missions movement started there. William Carey, considered by many to be the father of modern missions, was a British subject. Also, the eagle's wings would be part of the body of the empire, and when these wings were plucked this would represent a loss part of the empire.

The second beast would be Russia. Again, we find a familiar term, the Russian bear. "It was raised up on one side." From 1918 to the end of World War 2, Communist Russia didn't accomplish much. It "has three ribs in its mouth"; the last three victims, the Axis Powers, Germany, Italy, and Japan. "They said to it; arise, devour much flesh!" Immediately after the end of the second world war, Russia began conquering other nations. The rest is history. If we consider Persia to be the hear citing the fact that Persia had conquered three nations, we are ignoring the fact that after these conquests there was no "devouring much flesh." It is with Russia that we see this order of events unfold. Some have said that bears were very numerous in the area of Persia but the bear is a military description not an ecological one.

The third beast is not defined historically, yet, it has to be revealed in the near future. It cannot be any of the four empires of Daniel 2 i.e., Babylon (Iraq), Persia (Iran), Greece or Rome. Neither can it be either of the two just mentioned - Britain and Russia. It seems like the best candidate(s) will be found in the Orient. Since the beast has four heads and four wings it must be an alliance of four nations. It will strike from the air, apparently, with great speed. During the second world war the United Stated built air bases in China for the purposes of bombing Japan. The planes and their pilots were called "flying tigers." If my memory is correct, in September 1999 the Chinese had a parade in Beijing in which they showed some of their newest equipment. Among them was a newly designed and built bomber, they called it the "flying leopard bomber." It's anyone's guess who they will be allied with. A discussion of the meaning of two pictorial images "heads" and "horns" should be made here. In Daniel 7 the flying leopard has four head, in Daniel 8 that the goat (Greece) has four horns. In Revelation chapters 12, 13 and 17 we read of a beast with seven heads and ten horns; this will be dealt with in detail in a subsequent chapter. A careful observation of the use of these two images will reveal their differences; the heads are kings (or kingdoms) separate from each other which join together, whereas the horns are kings within the boundaries of an empire which may (Revelation 17), or may not (Daniel 11) be joined together. The one is external, the other is internal. In the case under consideration there will be four different nations which will be joined together in some sort of alliance,

It is important to note that all these empires (or remnants of them) will be in existence at the end time. In Daniel we read of the defeat of Babylon and Persia, and the breaking up of the Grecian Empire when its leader, Alexander the Great died, but no such thing is said about these three. Thus far history reveals the first two just gradually declined somewhat. Verse 12 says: "As for the rest of the beasts (the first three), they had their dominion taken away, yet their lives were prolonged for a season and a time."

Since verse 1 says Daniel had a dream and a vision in the first year of Belshazzar, king of Babylon, of four beasts which were coming, it's hard to believe that Babylon (under Belshazzar, not Nebuchadnezzar no less) would be the first beast. Babylon was nearing its conclusion. Chapter 8 of Daniel pictures Persia and Greece as a ram and a male goat, not as a bear and a flying leopard. In Dan, 7:3 Daniel sees four great beasts "each different from the other." There is not much difference between a ram and a male goat but there is a big difference between a bear and a flying leopard.

Finally, let us look at the book of Revelation which, as I stated before, ties together all the other prophecies, so we can get a clear, coherent picture. In chapters 12, 13, and 17, we read about beasts with seven heads and ten horns. They appear to refer to both the devil and the antichrist at the consummation of the age. It is generally acknowledged by prophecy commentators that the seven heads represent seven kingdoms (kings) down through history, and the ten horns are ten kings at the end time (see Rev.17: 10 - 12). In Revelation 13, we read of a beast (antichrist) who is the embodiment of all the Biblical kings and kingdoms of the past. In his description we have another evidence that the kings of Daniel 2 and Daniel 7 are not the same. Besides having the seven heads we read the following description:

> Rev. 13:2 "Now the beast which I saw was like a leopard, his feet were like the feet of a bear, and his mouth like the mouth of a lion......"

If the seven heads contain Babylon, Persia, and Greece; and the leopard, bear, and lion are also these three kingdoms, and then we have a duplication, but if the leopard, bear, and lion are three other kingdoms then this picture will make sense. More will said later in Chapter 12 about this.

CHAPTER 8

DANIEL CHAPTER 9

Daniel's 70 weeks are a key to understanding prophecy, and are contained in verses 24 - 27. They extend from the command to rebuild Jerusalem (under Persian rule after some Jews had returned) to the end of the so called tribulation period. The 70 weeks are 70 sevens of years, or 490 years. Those who hold to the premillenial, literal interpretation of Scripture believe there is a time break between the 69th and 70th weeks. A careful look at verses 26 & 27 will show that there are certain events which must take place between these two time periods. The destruction of Jerusalem (70 AD), and wars and desolations subsequent to that, for an undetermined period of time will take place. There have been translation and manuscript difficulties for these two verses, particularly the last half of verse 27.

Concerning verses 24 & 25 I have no differences with the standard interpretation of those who hold to the premillenial position. In translating the latter part of verse 26 there has been some disagreement among translators. The NKJV translates it this way; The end of it shall be with a flood and til the end of the war desolations are determined." Other translators think the words, "of the war," should be, "shall be war." I believe this makes a better connection between the first part of verse 26, which speaks of the destruction of the temple in 70 AD, and verse 27 which deals with the 70th week at the end time. The pronoun "he" of the statement,: "Then he shall confirm a covenant with many for one week," obviously refers back o the "prince who is to come" of the preceding verse. "He" also brings an end to sacrifice and offering in the middle of the week. But, who is he, other than the fact that he is a Roman Prince of the last days? It has been asserted that he is also the antichrist, by many (perhaps all) of the present day prophecy commentators. This text does not tell us that. The KJV continues to use the word "he" in the latter part of this verse, but the NKJV does not. Compare the two.

> KJV "And he shall confirm the covenant with many for one week; and in the midst of the week he shall cause the sacrifice and the oblation to cease, and for the overspreading of abominations he shall make it desolate, even until the consummation, and that determined shall be poured upon the desolate (or desolator)."

> NKJV "Then he shall confirm a covenant with many for one week; but in the middle of the week; he shall bring an end to sacrifice and offering, and on the wing of abominations shall be one who makes desolate, even until the consummation, which is determined, is poured out on the desolate (or desolator)."

Notice that "he shall make it desolate of the KJV becomes "one who makes desolate" in the NKJV. Other translators have made similar changes. Because of the long popularity of the KJV its wording has been the basis of many views we hold today. I am not running down the KJV; most of the Scriptures I have memorized have been from that translation, but here is one place I disagree with it. Since the KJV uses the word he to identify the one who desolates (or desecrates) the temple this would mean that the one who desolates the temple is the "prince who shall come," the Roman Prince, and he would have to be the antichrist. If, however, the change from "he" to "one" is correct then the antichrist would have to be someone else. Future discussions in this book will show the antichrist has to be someone else.

CHAPTER 9

THE HARLOT

We will be dealing here with Revelation chapter 17 & 18, which deals primarily with a harlot sitting on a scarlet beast with seven heads and ten horns. Many questions could be raised about the description and timing of this entity. She is called the mother of (spiritual) harlots and abominations of the earth. One gets the impression that all spiritual harlotry and abomination on earth are her offspring. But there is another side to her; there is much more said about her commercial success than her religious rebellion and deception. The three fold effect on mankind is stated in Rev. 18:3:

> "For all the nations have drunk of the wine of the wrath of the fornication, the kings of the earth have committed fornication with her, and the merchants of the earths have become rich through the abundance of her luxury.

I have counted at least sixteen verses in Jeremiah, Ezekiel, and Hosea which speak of Israel playing the harlot when worshiping other gods. All the commentators seem to agree this is what is meant by this woman being a harlot, a system which is totally anti-Christian and embraces the worship of any and every `false god. Some believe it will also include the erroneous worship of the God of the Bible, such as the cults and isms that surround us today. Since this is the mother of harlots it will embrace every false religious system in the world; do we not see a trend that way today spearheaded by liberalism?

In the ancient world, Tyre was a great commercial center which was temporarily destroyed by the Babylonians. See what Isaiah the prophet says about this city and its relationship to harlotry.

> Is. 23:15 - 17 "Now it shall come to pass in that day that Tyre will be forgotten seventy years, according to the days of one king. At the end of seventy years, it will happen to Tyre as in the song of the harlot:
>
> 'Take a harp, go about the city,
>
> You forgotten harlot;
>
> Make sweet melody, sing many songs,
>
> That you may be remembered.'
>
> And it shall be, at the end of seventy years,
>
> that the Lord will visit Tyre. She will return
>
> to her pay, and commit fornication with all
>
> the kingdoms of the world on the face of the earth."

Strange, how commercial success can be compared with harlotry and fornication, but this appears to be the case. This fits right in with the description of the harlot of Revelation 17 & 18.

There has been much speculation about mystery Babylon; what it will be, and when it will be. Some have equated it with the Roman Catholic Church; others see it as a false religious conglomerate with the Roman Church as its head; still others see it as I have described it, simply an all-embracing multifaceted false religious system. Some think it will be located in Rome, others believe it will be in Babylon, still others see it as a large, heavily populated, coastal, commercial city with many different religious systems, that evolves into what is described in Revelation. Some believe it will be in the first half of the 70th week and destroyed by the beast in, or at the end of that period.

The woman is said to be a mystery, something never before revealed, but could it be the result of what the Apostle Paul said in II Thes.2:3 "Let no one deceive you by any means for that Day will not come unless the falling away comes first"? With orthodoxy (of various types) losing its influence and with the departure of the saints at the rapture the door will be wide open for something like this. It doesn't seem likely that entity like this could come into being overnight so we should look for signs of its origination in our day. Its influence appears to be practiced worldwide. She sits on many waters, which are interpreted to be "peoples, multitudes, nations, and tongues." Rev. 18:3 previously quoted speaks of all the nations, the kings of the earth, and the merchants of the earth being closely connected with her. Not all the kings of the earth are said to "hate the harlot" and, eventually; make her desolate and naked, eat her flesh and burn her with fire." Consider a few verses from Revelation 17:

> Rev. 17: 12 "And the ten horns which you saw are ten kings who have received authority for one hour as kings with the beast."

> Rev. 17:13 "These are of one mind, and they will give their power and authority on the beast."

> Rev. 17:16 "And the ten horns which you saw on the beast, these will hate the harlot, make her desolate and naked, eat her flesh and burn her with fire."

Rev. 17:17 "For God has put into their hearts to fulfill His purpose, to be of one mind, and to give their kingdom to the beast, until the words of God are fulfilled."

I see three important things taught here.

1. The harlot precedes the establishment of the revival of the Roman Empire.

2. The harlot serves as a catalyst for the reviving of the Roman Empire.

3. The destruction of the harlot paves the way for the revived Roman Empire under the leadership of the beast to come into being.

Most prophetic teaching that I have heard place the harlot in the same time period as the revived Roman Empire, but having her destroyed sometime during that period of Roman (beast) rule. The harlot and the beast are mortal enemies and they cannot both be ruling at the same time. In verse 3 the woman is pictured as seated on the beast, and she is portrayed in all her glory while being in that position. In the image of Daniel 2 the feet and toes (10 kings) are pictured as iron and clay which cannot mix, and we are told that even intermarriage was not able to make them mix; but here in Revelation 17 we are told that "God has put into their hearts to fulfill His purpose, to be of one mind, and to give their kingdom to the beast." That which was not possible before the arrival of the harlot and the beast has now become a reality. These are ten kings "who have received no kingdom as yet, but they receive authority for one hour as kings with the beast."

There are other reasons for believing the harlot precedes the beast coming to power. The beast comes to power. The beast comes to power as the first horseman of Revelation 6 riding out conquering on a white horse. As we continue reading that portion we discover the calamity of all out warfare with its attendant death and destruction. By the time we get to the fourth horseman we read of one fourth of the world's population being stain. How many more will be injured and how much property will be destroyed? When we compare this with the description of the world's condition in Revelation 18 at the time of the harlots greatest influence, we see exact opposites. Such commercial prosperity and religious unity would make such a good candidate for that tome spoken in I Thes. 5:3, a time of "peace and safety." It could also be described with the words in Luke 17 :

> Luke 17: 27 & 28 "They ate, they drank, they married wives, they were given in marriage until the day that Noah entered the ark ....Likewise as it was also I the days of Lot. They ate, they drank, they bought, they sold, they planted, they built," until " the day that Lot went out of Sodom."

It would seem to be a wonderful time to live; the calm before the storm. The fact that Babylon is not mentioned until late in Revelation, the first time briefly in chapter 14 and later more extensively in chapters 17 & 18, is no reason to believe that it comes late in the prophetic scenario. The trumpet judgments, which include seas turning to blood and ships destroyed as a result of this, are all treated in chapter prior to this. Also, the rule of the beast is not mentioned until chapter 13 after many judgments are discussed, some during his rise to power and some after.

The description of the destruction of Babylon seems to meet all the criteria for a nuclear annihilation. One must wonder what reaction there will be from the other nations who realize the ten kings of the revived Roman Empire under the leadership of the beast have done this. Consider the following verses:

> Rev. 18:9 - 11 "And the kings of the earth who committed fornication and lived luxuriously with her

will weep and lament for her when they see the smoke of her burning, standing at a distance for fear of her torment, saying, 'Alas, alas, that great city Babylon, that mighty city! For in one hour your judgment has come,' and the merchants of the earth will weep and mourn over her, for no one buys their merchandise anymore."

Rev. 18:15 - 19 "The merchants of these things, who became rich by her, will stand at a distance for fear of her torment, weeping and wailing, and saying 'Alas, alas, that great city that was clothed in fine linen, purple, and scarlet, and adorned with gold and precious stones and pearls! For in one hour such great riches came to nothing.' And every shipmaster, all who traveled by ship, sailors, and as many as trade on the sea, stood at a distance and cried out when they saw the smoke of her burning, saying, 'What is like this great city?' And they threw dust on their heads and cried out, weeping and wailing, and saying, 'Alas, alas, the great city, in which all who had ships on the sea became rich by her wealth! For in one hour she is made desolate."

Does this trigger the events of Revelation 6 and Daniel 11, where we read of the wars and conquests of the beast? It would seem logical that there would be some reaction by other nations who were so intimately with the harlot city.

In recent years, there have been gatherings of the various world religions in major cities in Europe and the United States. There was a call for a United Religions on the west coast just as we have a United Nations in New York. There was a rumor a few years ago of the establishment of such an entity in Florida. But we must remember that Mystery Babylon is not just a religious establishment, but also a world trade center (sound familiar?). In order for the harlot, as described in Revelation, to come into existence every form of Christian orthodoxy must be minimized or eliminated. Apostasy has made big inroads into Protestantism due to the invasion of liberalism. Some high officials in the Catholic Church have stated their prophetic view that the last Pope will be an apostate. Makes one wonder about the false prophet of Revelation who has "two horns like a lamb and spoke like a dragon." It is my personal conviction that liberalism is our biggest enemy today, having become firmly entrenched in just about every phase of American life. Liberalism appears to be predicted for latter times in 2 Tim 3:5 and 2 Peter 3:4. I see three stages in latter times prophecy: liberalism (although not prophesied) religious harlotry, and the reign of the antichrist, as the world goes from bad, to worse, to worse yet.

Although the harlot is not a military force yet there must be a minor military or police for "in her was found the blood of prophets and saints, and of all who were slain on the earth." A strange verse is found in Rev. 18:20 "Rejoice over her, O heaven, and you holy apostles and prophets, for God has avenged you on her!" Is this a consummation of centuries of anti-God religions finally achieving its goal of united opposition to God's people. (Compare Matt. 23:35). At the recent various gatherings of the world religions, every religious group seemed to be welcome except the evangelicals. Although this internationally approved harlot will be blasphemous hateful, and violent, it appears that some of God's people will be able to live right in the middle of it (like Lot living in Sodom).

> Rev. 18:4 "And I heard another voice from heaven saying, 'Come out of her, my people, lest you share in her sins, and lest you receive of her plagues.'"

Perhaps they will not be very outspoken about their faith. The influence, or power, of this organized religious, commercial entity is shown in the following:

> Rev. 17:18 "And the woman who you saw is that great city which reigns over the kings of the earth."

After the physical destruction of Babylon it comes to a fitting end: "Babylon the great is fallen, is fallen, and has become a habitation of demons, a prison for every foul spirit, and a cage for every unclean and hated bird." (Rev. 18:2). A final thought on Babylon, if the U.S. turns out to be the nation where Babylon is located (I think it will) then we can expect to see a worsening of relations with certain European and middle eastern nations. Also, although the destruction of Babylon appears to be the result of a nuclear attack, it is evident that most weapons of mass destruction will have been destroyed since what we have today would wipe out the world's population in a few days, but in the descriptions of the wars of the apocalypse (described also in the latter verses of Daniel 11) one fourth of the worlds population will be destroyed in that period of time.

I believe the timing of the harlot will parallel the timing of the Israel agreement, for apparently how could there be such worldwide peace and agreement? The destruction of Babylon would then lead to the "wars and rumours of wars" described by the first four seals of Revelation 6. I believe the 5th seal parallels the trumpet and bowl judgements.

CHAPTER 10

IMMINENCY

Most pretibultaion writers believe imminency to be the most important reason for holding their position. They cite such passages as: I Cor. 1:7; Phil. 3:20; 4:5; I Thes. 1:10; Titus 2:13; Heb. 9:28; James 5:7 - 9; I Peter 1:13; Jude 21; Rev. 3:11; 22:7, 12 & 20. Most of these verses emphasize looking and waiting expectantly for the return of Christ, and what will accompany His return. There are seven exceptions to this. Phil. 4:5 and James 5:8 say that the Lord is at hand; James 5:9 says the Lord is standing at the door; the verses in Revelation all emphasize the idea that the Lord is coming quickly, speedily, or soon. A question must be raised here. Does it seem logical to think that for 19 1/2 centuries (so far) men are to be instructed from the Scriptures to anxiously look and hope for the return of Christ, to believe He is at hand, at the door, and will soon return? But, you say, the Scriptures teach that, and are infallible. I agree, but I think there are some other factors that should be considered.

In the first century church Christ was not a distant memory, but His life, death, resurrection were all a very recent happening. The apostles, who basically started the early church, had been in His presence for over 3 1/2 years, and sorely missed Him; consequently they were given the "Comforter." It was only natural to eagerly await His reappearing. Some may disagree with me, but it is my persuasion that the disciples (including Paul) had limited understanding of the prophetic Scriptures concerning the second coming, and, it seems, a slight misunderstanding of those Scriptures. In those days, the Roman Empire was at its peak and there was a temple in Jerusalem. In our days we look for a revival of the old Roman Empire and a rebuilding of the temple (for the antichrist to desecrate). In their thinking the stage was set for the return of Christ; we look for the setting of the stage for His return. They may have understood Dan. 9:27 but they did not understand Dan. 9:26. they knew about the antichrist, the "abomination of desolation" from the Olivet discourse and Paul's second letter to the Thessalonians, and the destruction of the temple, also from the teachings of Christ just prior to the Olivet discourse on the second coming. What they did not understand was the fact that it was their present temple that would be destroyed, but a second rebuilt temple that would be desecrated. In Matthew 24 after the disciples were told of the destruction of the temple - not one stone left standing on another - they then asked the question:

> Matt. 24:3 "Tell us, when will these things be? And what will be the sign of Your coming, and of the end of the age?"

The three things mentioned here, "These things," "Your coming," and the "end of the age" were, in their minds, events that would all happen at approximately the same time. The Olivet discourse Prophetic Portion, however, contains no reference to the destruction of the temple in either Matthew or Mark's Gospel. Since their understanding precluded any time period between the destruction of the temple and the "abomination of desolation," then the stage appeared to be set for end times events, as they perceived them, and therefore, it was appropriate for them to be eagerly looking for the return of the Lord. In fact, it would be very inappropriate for them not to be doing so. In our day, we watch current events to see how close we feel we are to the end, and much prophetic preaching has been done as a result of this.

One might ask the question, "How do you know they had such a misunderstanding of prophecy?" My answer is this: imminency is taught in Paul's letters; but if he knew the then, present, temple had to be destroyed, the Jews scattered, then regathered, and another temple built for the end time, how could he have told them to be eagerly looking for the return of the Lord, for these things would have to happen first? The very idea of imminency precludes the possibility of anything to happen before the return of the Lord. It is worth remembering that the disciples were sent out to preach the kingdom of heaven was at hand. It was, but it was not. James 5:8 says "The coming of the Lord is at hand." Some may be objecting what I am writing but, remember, 19 1/2 centuries have gone by since that was written, Isiah 11:11 tells us "the Lord shall set His hand again the second time to recover the remnant of His people." Biblical history records only once recovering of the Jewish people by the time of the apostles, therefore, there remains another recovering of God's people in the future.

Luke's Gospel. Though not containing the Olivet discourse, nevertheless, does contain in two discourses information bearing on the questions the disciples asked in Matthew 24. the are contained in chapters 17 and 21. The prophecy jumps back and forth, end times and apostolic times. In Luke 17, verses 2- 24 are end times prophecy, verse 25 immediate future, then verses 26 - 37 end times again. In Luke 21, verses 8 - 11 end times prophecy, verses 12 - 24 near future, and verses 25 - 36 are again end times prophecy. It is my contention they were not able to see these distinctions clearly. Even today there are some Bible commentators who do not seem to be able to see them. The point of it all is this; the two fold invasion of Jerusalem seemed to blur their prophetic vision. If the apostle Paul had a clear understanding of this how could he possibly have written, " ....eagerly waiting for the revelation of our Lord Jesus Christ?" (I Cor. 1:7), but this is for us.

I think after 70 AD the early Christians had to rethink the prophetic ideas. Some early church fathers proposed the 7th - 1000 years kingdom age. John, the youngest of the apostles, wrote his Gospel, letters, and Revelation after 70 AD. There is no Olivet discourse in his Gospel but a two verse (John 14:2 & 3) revelation of the rapture. In Matthew's Gospel the Olivet discourse deals only with events of the 70th week of Daniel but the parables seem to refer to the rapture. Mark's Gospel devotes one verse (Mark 13:9) to the apostolic age and the rest to the 70th week: Luke's Gospel makes clear cut distinctions in prophetic material between the apostolic age, including the destruction of the temple and scattering of the Jews, and the end time. John's Gospel speaks of the rapture. There appears to be a progression in prophetic revelation through the four Gospels.

John's letters, written after 70 AD, do not exhort his readers to await eagerly the return of the Lord, but rather he takes a different approach.

> John 2:18 "Little children, it is the last hour; and as you have heard that the antichrist is coming, even now many antichrists have come, by which we know that it is the last hour."

Once again we are confronted with the problem of the last hour lasting 19 1/2 ; most commentators are content to let it be that way. I believe John was writing (under inspiration) to readers in his day with a limited knowledge of prophecy. The principle that John stated was true and is applicable to us today, as is also Paul's exhortation to look for the return of the Lord. Consider the conditions of the world. The Jews are back in the land, desperately in need of a peace treaty, the revival of the Roman Empire appears to be under way, and there are 1.2 billion Muslims who say "God has no son!" ("He is antichrist who denies the Father and the Son" I John 2:22). Are we being instructed properly in these latter times?

Those who hold to the view of imminency should consider what the apostle Peter says in his second letter:

> 2 Pet. 3:12 "Looking for and hastening the coming of the day of God, because of which the heavens will be dissolved being on fire, and the elements will melt with fervent heat."

Here we are exhorted to be looking for and hastening the coming of a day which will be at least 1,007 <u>plus</u> years after the rapture. How can this be I we apply the doctrine of imminency here? Many future events must occur before this can happen. Isn't it possible to look forward to something that is off in the distant future? We have two choices here; either we throw away the idea of imminency altogether or accept the incomplete prophetic knowledge of the writer and his readers. Take your pick. If imminency is true then surely this verse should be a good example of it, for it has two exhortations, "looking for" and "hastening the coming of," to cause us to think of the "day of the God" being near and imminent.

In the first chapter of Acts, at the time of the ascension, the disciples asked the following question:

> Acts 1:6 "....Lord, will You at this time restore the kingdom to Israel?"

Obviously, the disciples had no understanding of the Olivet discourse whatsoever, or any other end time prophecy they were taught by Christ in His life here and in the 40 days after the resurrection. If the disciples (including Paul) knew so much about prophecy why was the Apostle John commissioned to write the book of Revelation a quarter of a century after the destruction of Jerusalem? As Daniel was finishing his book he was told to "shut up the words, and seal the book until the time of the end;" (Dan.

12:4), but as John was finishing the book of Revelation he was told "Do not seal the words of the prophecy of this book." The book of Revelation is our guide to a full understanding of prophecy. It was written decades after most of the apostles had passed from the scene.

Some will fear that what I have said is a denial of inspiration. Such is not the case. The inspired writers were kept from errors in doctrine and historical data, but what we are considering are words of exhortation based on the (then) current knowledge of prophecy. It was proper for Paul to exhort them to look eagerly for the return of Christ, and in our day it would be wise to consider such exhortations as we watch the unfolding of world events. If the idea of imminency, and consequently pretribulation rapturism, was set forth in the first century it would still be a valid argument today, even though the idea of imminency would not be valid down through the centuries.

There are other problems to be found in Revelation chapter 22 that those who like to understand the Bible could meditate on, and ask for illumination, that they might have better understanding. In verse 10 it says "the time is at hand." In verse 7, 12, & 20, where Christ is speaking, we read "I am coming quickly (speedily, shortly, soon)." How long a time do the words "at hand" and "soon" imply?

An after thought I had after finishing this chapter. There have been many quotations from Paul quoted to prove imminency but what about Peter? Peter could not possibly have believed in imminency because he was told by Christ Himself by what death he would glorify God (John 21:18 & 19). Perhaps this is why Peter exhorted his followers to be "looking for and hastening" an event which would occur long after their departure from earth (one way or another). Also, consider the misunderstanding about the Apostle John living to see the return of Christ (John 21:32 - 24); no wonder they looked for a soon return of Christ and so exhorted believers to be waiting expectantly for Him.

CHAPTER 11

JOEL'S PROPHECY

The book of Joel is to me a strange book in that it appears, in some respects, to be quite different from the other prophetic books. A standard interpretation is that for most of the first two chapters the subject is the invasion of locusts in Joel's time, the distress of the people, their crying out to God, their repentance and their consequent deliverance from this plague. The next two verses tell of the pouring out of the Spirit at some time later in history. This is followed by three verses introducing us to the end time, day of the Lord events. Four and one half of these five verses are quoted by Peter on the day of Pentecost. The remaining third chapter discusses the day of the Lord judgment of the Gentile nations and the deliverance of Israel at that time.

After much thought, I have decided not to present a view toward which I lean, but cannot be dogmatic about, but rather to present various bits of information generally overlooked, and allow the reader to make up his or her own mind. The date of this book is uncertain, with some commentators favoring an early date (majority view) while others favor a later date. In light of this consider the following:

Joel 1:2 & 3 "Hear this, you elders, and give ear, all you inhabitants of the land! Has anything like this happened in your days, or even in the days of your fathers? Tell your children about it, let your children tell their children, and their children another generation."

Joel 2:2 "......A people [locusts] come, great and strong, the like of whom has never been; nor will there ever be any such after them, even for many successive generations.

How could this catastrophic event escape the pages of history? We find it neither in Biblical (except here) or secular history. If we knew when this happened we would be able to date this book very precisely. Not only was it one of a kind event but the remembrance of it was to be preserved from generation to generation. Other events, such as Passover, are recorded and celebrated each year; why not this one?

Another missing piece of information which we could expect to find is missing from the book itself. As we progress through the book, we read of the extent of the calamity of locusts, fire and drought; the people are called to cry to the Lord; the nearness of the final, total, destruction of the land; the call to repentance; and, strangely, the next portion of His promise (present tense - is it past or future?). What is missing? If this is a historical as well as prophetic book, why don't we read of the reaction of the people to this call to repentance before reading of their deliverance?

In the call to repentance we read the following:

Joel 2:12 & 13 "Now, therefore, says the Lord, turn to me with all your heart, with fasting, with weeping, and with mourning, so rend your heart, and not your garments; return to the Lord your God......"

What is their sin? When we look at any of the other prophetic books, whether it be about Israel or any of the nations, the specific nature of their sin(s) is always mentioned. When I read about their weeping and mourning I am reminded of the following passage from Zechariah.

> Zech. 12:10 - 14 "And I will pour on the house of David and on the inhabitants of Jerusalem. The Spirit of grace and supplication, then they will look on Me whom they have pierced; they will mourn for HIM as one mourns for his only son, and grieve for Him as one grieves for a firstborn. In that day there shall be a great mourning in Jerusalem, like the mourning at Hadad Rimmon in the plain of Megiddo. And the land shall mourn, every family by itself......all the families that remain, every family by itself, and their wives by themselves.

We will deal with this a little more, later in this chapter.

Let us deal with two (actually three) brief statements the Lord makes about His people, Israel.

> Joel 2; 19 "....I will no longer (no more) make you a reproach among the nations."

> Joel 2: 26 "....My people shall never be put to shame."

> Joel 2: 27 ".....My people shall never be put to shame."

If this event took place 2800 years ago these statements could not be true. What about the Babylonian invasion, the Syrian invasion, the Roman invasion and the consequent dispersion of the Jews for 1900 years after that?

Toward the end of the second chapter a portion quoted by Peter on the day of Pentecost is found. There has been much discussion on this portion. Verse 28 says:

> Joel 2: 29 "And it shall come to pass afterward that I will pour out My Spirit on all flesh; your sons and your daughters shall prophesy, your old men shall dream dreams, your young men shall see visions."

It is my view that "afterward" refers to the kingdom age. Peter did not specifically say that the experience they had on the day of Pentecost was a fulfillment of Joel's prophecy but "this is what was spoken by the Prophet Joel." He included verses which will be fulfilled in that latter time we call Daniel's 70th week. A similar situation is found in the fifteenth chapter of Acts where, at the Jerusalem Council, there was a discussion about Jews and Gentiles being saved by faith, both equal terms. James quotes from the Prophet Amos a portion dealing with the kingdom age to show that the Gentiles would be called to faith in God. Before he quotes the Prophet Amos he says, "And with this the words of the prophets agree, just as it is written." He does not say that what was happening was a fulfillment of the Prophet Amos. We should also note that Joel says nothing about speaking in tongues (although this happened in the early church. The Prophet Joel says very specifically:

> Joel 2:28 "….Your sons and your daughters shall prophesy, your old men shall dream dreams, your young men shall see visions."

Apparently the purpose for pouring out of the Spirit in the kingdom age will be for future revelations. There are some who believe the pouring out of the Spirit will begin in the tribulation period just before the kingdom age; this is possible. Others have taught that for the book to have chronological sequence the locust plague must precede the pouring out of the Spirit at Pentecost; afterwards conditions in the tribulation period are described (chapters 2: 30 - 32); then the latter part of the tribulation followed by a brief description of the kingdom age at the end of chapter 3. but it must be noted that verses 4 - 8 of chapter 3 are ancient history.

Let's compare some verses in the locust plague section with verses in the description of the end of the age (chapter 3).

> Joel 2:10 "The earth quakes before them, the heavens tremble."

> Joel 3:16 "….the heavens and earth will shake."

> Joel 2:10 "…The sun and moon grow dark, and the stars diminish their brightness."

> Joel 3:15 "The sun and moon will grow dark, and the stars will diminish their brightness."

> Joel 2:27 "Then you shall know that I am in the midst of Israel, and that I am the Lord your God."

> Joel 3:17 "So you shall know that I am the Lord your God dwelling in Zion My holy mountain."

In addition to the plague of locusts Joel also mentions drought and burning of vegetation. In Revelation there is a 3 1/2 year drought and some of the judgments describe worldwide burning of grass and trees.

Previously I mentioned there was no specific sin (s) which Israel was accused of and from which they should repent. Let's look at the very end of the book for another clue in this matter.

> Joel 3:21 "For I will acquit them of bloodguilt, whom I had not acquitted."

Now consider Matthew's Gospel:

> Matt. 27:25 "And all the people answered and said, 'His blood be on us and on our children.'" Read that verse from Joel again.:

Joel 3:21 "For I will acquit them of bloodguilt, whom I
had not acquitted."

I intended that last line to be my last line for this chapter,
but as in other previous chapter some new thoughts came to me
which I think should be included. I shall attempt a rather difficult
explanation of an idea which revolves around one word in a verse
in Joel, chapter 2.

Joel 2:28 "And it shall come to pass afterward that I
will pour out My Spirit on all flesh."

The key word is "afterward.." I am not a Hebrew scholar but
after having checked several references using this word I see that it
is used in the sense of immediately, soon, or shortly after. We would
get the same impression for the use of the English word "afterward.."
If this would not be the case then why not use expressions such as
are used elsewhere in Joel?

Joel 3:1 "For, behold, in those days and at that time...."

Joel 3:18 "And it will come to pass in that day..."

The point of it all is this: the events described in the preceding
verses must be near in time to those described in verse 28. the
preceding verses describe the restoration of the land after the locusts,
drought and fire caused great destruction. If that destruction and
restoration happened eight centuries before Christ and if verse 28
refers to the day of Pentecost there would be 8 1/2 centuries in
between. If verse 28 refers to a time either in the latter part of the
tribulation or some time later in the kingdom age there would be
close to three millennia (depending on when the Lord returns).
If, however, the events preceding verse 28 are end time events,
it would be proper to use the word "afterward," if we accept the
interpretation that verse 28 refers to some time in the kingdom age.

Another idea to be examined is continuity and coherency. One scenario would look like this. The text up to Chapter 2, verse 27 describes the destruction and restoration of the land of Israel and Israel regaining God's favor about eight centuries before Christ. The next two verses describe either the day of Pentecost (8 1/2 centuries later), or a time 2,000 years after that (or more). The next three verses appear to describe the 6th seal of Revelation 6 some time during the last 3 1/2 years of Daniel's 70th week. Chapter three which follows then describes the judgment of the Gentile nations and the deliverance of Israel, followed by a brief description of kingdom age conditions. Another scenario will be like this. The text up to chapter 2, verse 27 describes Israel's disciplinary punishment, repentance and restoration in the last days (Daniel's 70th week). this is followed by the pouring out of the Spirit some time after that during the kingdom age. In chapter 2, from verse 30 on we read about the Gentile nations. Notice verse 32: "And it shall come to pass that whatsoever calls on the name of the Lord shall be saved." The Apostle Paul quotes this in Romans 10:13 applying the principle of it in the church age, and emphasizing the unity of Jew and Gentile in this age. This introduces us to the end time judgment of the Gentiles which is the primary topic of chapter three. Chapter three concludes with a description of the blessings on Israel in the kingdom age but Egypt and Edom are described as a "desolation." The book concludes with "For the Lord dwells in Zion." This scenario then describes Israel's judgment and destruction of the Gentile nations in that same period; then the conditions of both in the kingdom age. I leave it to the reader to decide which of the two scenarios look best. At the beginning of this chapter I said I could not be dogmatic about a certain view I lean toward, and I guess it has become obvious I believe that the prophet who will proclaim this message will not be Joel. This view would mean that all four references to the Day of the Lord in Joel would refer to the same time, i.e., the climax of the tribulation period. The last verse of Joel tells us why judgment had been necessary "For I will acquit them of bloodguilt whom I had not acquitted.

CHAPTER 12

SEVEN HEADS AND TEN HORNS

There are many mysteries and much pictorial imagery used in prophecy. The secrets, the revelations, do not yield to man's intellect. It is illumination of man's mind by the Spirit of God that enables men to come to an accurate understanding of the prophetic Scriptures and, in fact, a true understanding of all the important doctrines, contained therein. Humbleness of mind and extreme caution should be exercised in our search, and dogmatism need not be proclaimed in every area, particularly in prophecy. There is much in prophecy of which we can be certain. They are under consideration has brought forth much controversy, though there is considerable agreement in certain areas.

The place to start our search should be in the second chapter of Daniel. Many readers will be familiar with this portion which tells us about an image which King Nebuchadnezzar saw in a dream. It is an image of a man made of four different metals, gold, silver, bronze, iron, and the feet being a mixture of iron and clay. The metals are in that order starting from the head coming down to the feet. Daniel interprets the dream to the king and tells him the four different metals represent four different kingdoms, starting with the king's own kingdom of Babylon, after which will come three others that we know to be Persia, Greece and Rome. The book itself reveals Persia and Greece to be the next kingdoms and we know from history, as well as the New Testament, that Rome is the fourth. In today's world Babylon would be equivalent to Iraq, and Persia changed its name to Iran. A king representing each one of these kingdoms would give us four kings, which would be the equivalent to four of the seven heads. We know from Revelation 17:10 that the seven heads are seven kings. This same appears to tell us there will be a second king coming out of the Roman Empire (in the future), which would give us five kings or heads. We are told in Dan. 2:44 that the ten toes are ten kings in the latter time of the kingdom of iron (Rome). We know the heads are kings representing kingdoms but the toes are kings of a divided kingdom in latter times, which cannot get together because of political differences in their respective countries. We know, however, from Revelation 17:13 & 17 these kings ultimately become united under the "beast" (antichrist), and that kingdom (final version of Rome) will be destroyed by Christ at His second coming (Daniel 2:44 & 45). When we move to Daniel 7 we will see that the ten toes of Daniel 2 are the same as the ten horns of Daniel 1, and, consequently, the same ten horns of Revelation, chapters 12, 13, and 17.

In Daniel 7, which was dealt with in a previous chapter, we find four beasts, the fourth of which will be the last kingdom (verses 11, 22, 26) before the Messianic age. Verse 7 tells us it had 10 horns, and verse 24 that the ten horns are ten kings, therefore we know that the ten horns are the ten kings of the final (Roman) Empire. We have now identified five heads and ten horns. The information thus far presented in this chapter is a standard presentation of facts generally agreed upon by those of the pretribulation rapture position.

The identification of the two remaining heads have been asserted by most commentators to be ancient Egypt (Exodus) and Assyria (2 Kings). Both of these kingdoms with their respective kings preceded Babylon, and were not included in the image of Daniel 2. The question then is: should we go back before Babylon to find the two other heads (kings) of the seven headed and ten horned beast of Revelation or should we look in Daniel for two other possible candidates? My view is we should look in Daniel, for we are introduced to the idea of Gentile world dominion (Israel included) in the image of Daniel 2. In the days of ancient Egypt Israel had not yet become a nation in their own land, and the Assyrians never conquered the southern kingdom of Judah. It was not until King Nebuchadnezzar of Babylon came on the scene that the nation of Israel was captured and the first Gentile world power was established. The seven heads of Revelation cannot be seven kings of different world powers, since Daniel 2 makes it clear there will only before. We have already determined that a fifth king is from the reviving Roman Empire which gives us two kings from one empire. The seven heads of Revelation must be recognized as seven kings representing seven kingdoms which subjugated Israel beginning with Babylon. When we say seven kingdoms we mean five kingdoms and ancient and future Rome. Thus far, if we do not include ancient Egypt and Assyria, we have only three kingdoms and ancient and future Rome. I believe Daniel gives us the other two kingdoms. After the death of Alexander the Great his Grecian Empire was divided four ways according to the compass; north, east, south, and west. The book of Daniel is concerned only with two of them; the king of the south (Egypt) and the king of the north (Syria). We are introduced to them in chapter 8, and chapter 11 gives considerable information about them The king of the south (Egypt) of the second and third century BC is not to be confused with Ancient Egypt at the time of the exodus, nor should the king of the north (Syria) be confused with the Syrians of 2 Kings. It can be observed in our present world that the kingdom of Assyria no longer exists, but there still remain remnants (countries) of all the other kingdoms.

The seven heads and ten horns are found in Revelation chapter 12, 13 and 17 but their different identification is found in Daniel. The ten horns portion are explained as ten kings of the last empire in both Daniel and Revelation, but the seven heads are found only in Revelation, but must be identified from the information contained in Daniel. In Revelation 12, we read about a fiery red dragon having seven heads and ten horns; the red dragon being identified as the Devil. In Revelation 13 we read of a beast rising up out of the sea, having seven heads and ten horns, henceforth referred to as the beast or antichrist. The dragon has seven crowns on its heads while the beast has ten crowns on its horns. Revelation 12:7 says the Devil deceives the whole world, and in the fourth chapter of Luke the Devil showed Christ all the kingdoms of the world in a moment of time and said, "All this authority I will give You, and their glory; for this has been delivered to me, and I give it to whomever I wish." This explains why the dragon has the crowns on his heads, for those kingdoms were his. The beast will be the last world ruler being given authority over the kingdoms of the ten kings as shown in Revelation 17:

> Rev. 17:16, 17 "And the ten horns which you saw on the beast, these will hate the harlot, make her desolate and naked, eat her flesh and burn her with fire, for God has put it into their hearts to fulfill His purpose to be of one mind, and to give their kingdoms to the beast........."

This explains why the beast has the ten crowns on his ten horns. To understand the reason for the differences between the dragon and the beast we must realize the dragon's primary purpose is persecuting or subjugating the nation Israel; consequently his body is different from that of the beast in chapter 13. The beast is more interested in world dominion and its body involves three more kingdoms- Britain, Russia and probably, China (with three allies). These three kingdoms were not (and will not be) involved in the conquest of the nation of Israel.

Now, we move to the scarlet colored beast of chapter 17. this beast has no crowns at all. The reason is that we see here in a fetal stage the coming kingdom of the beast; the harlot is holding it back at this time. In verse 13 we read:

Rev. 17:13 "And the ten horns which you saw are ten kings who have received no kingdom as yet........."

But when these kings "give their power and authority to the beast" (Rev. 17:13) then the nondescript, scarlet colored beast becomes the beast of Revelation 13 with the ten crowns on his ten horns.

Revelation 17 gives us insight into the mystery of the beast with the seven heads and ten horns. Before going into this let me say that I do not believe the seven heads are the seven hills of Rome. This would negate everything we have said so far on the subject. Verse 9 says "the seven heads are seven mountains," and verse 10 continues "There are also seven kings." Babylon has been described as a mountain (Jer. 51:25) and the kingdom of Christ as a mountain that filled the whole earth (Dan. 2:35). What do the seven hills of Rome have to do with seven kings, even the Caesars? Would the seven hills of Rome have seven crowns on them? Why would the crowns be removed when we move from the dragon to the beast? How many Caesars were there? Why only one more Caesar predicted after the one ruling in John's day? The dragon of chapter 12 and the beast of chapter 13 are shown with seven heads and ten horns; what would seven hills and seven Caesars have to do with the prophecy? To be able to identify the seven mountains with Rome would require us to have extra- Biblical geological knowledge of the city of Rome. Most of the Caesars of ancient Rome are not mentioned in the Bible, therefore, we would need extra- Biblical knowledge of history to be able to identify them by name and number. The beast has a composite body of the beasts mentioned in Daniel 7 as well as the ten horns mentioned there. The heads could not be identified anywhere in Daniel or, for that matter, not in Revelation either until we get to Rev. 17:9. But according to Daniel 2 the other kingdoms preceding the Roman Empire are to be in existence and to be destroyed at the time when Christ returns. Why would they not be represented at the time when Christ returns. Why would they not be represented in the imagery of the last times? It seems to me that those who hold to the ten hills of Rome theory want to involve the Roman Catholic Church in end times prophecy.

Let's have a further inquiry into the beast of Revelation 13 and make a comparison with the beast of Revelation 17. Let's compare three similar, yet different, statements from each chapter.

> Rev. 13:3 "I saw one of his heads as if it had been mortally wounded, and his deadly wound was healed."

> Rev. 13;12 "…….and those who dwell in it to worship the first beast, whose deadly wound was healed.'

> Rev. 13:14 "…….telling those who dwell on the earth to make an image to the beast who was wounded by the sword and lived."

> Rev. 17:18 "The beast that you saw was, and is not, and will ascend out of the bottomless pit and go to perdition……."

> Rev. 17:8 "…..when they see the beast was, and is not, and yet is."

> Rev. 17:11 "And the beast that was, and is not, is himself also the eighth ……"

The fact of a triple emphasis makes this very important, and I may say, very intriguing. Chapter 13 tells of a man who was seen, by those of that future time, slain, and then come back to life again. Chapter 17, as we shall see, tells of a man who long ago died and has come back. The fact that it was said to John "he was and is not" indicates he died before John's time.

Again, let us make some comparisons.

> Rev. 17:8 "The beast that you saw was, and is not, and will ascend out of the bottomless pit ……"

Rev. 17:10 & 11 "There are also seven kings. Five have fallen, one is, and the other has not yet come. And when he comes, he must continue a short time. And the beast that was, and is not, is himself also the eighth, and is of the seven, and is going to perdition."

Do you see the parallel?:

"The beast that you saw was" compared to "Five have fallen"

"And is not" compared to "One is"

"Will ascend out of the bottomless pit" compared to

"Is himself, also the eighth" (the seventh comes for a short time just before the eighth)

Doesn't it appear that "the beast that you saw was" out of the "five (who) have fallen?" But what about chapter 13 that tells us that the people of his (future) day will see him resurrected? The answer to this puzzling question lies in verse 11. The translation I have been using (NKJV) says he "is of the seven." Other translators have said "one of the seven." but this is not correct. The Greek word used here is ek .which means "out of," so what are we being told here is, he is "out of the seven." Every word of the scriptures is inspired and must not be taken lightly. I believe king number seven is the Roman Prince of Daniel 9:27 who confirms (strengthens) the covenant between Israel and her enemies, and later causes Israel to stop her sacrifices and offerings. It is my guess that an irate, orthodox Jew will be the one who slays him. He will come back to life - or will he? His body will, but one from the past will indwell it. If you think this is ridiculous then why does it say "he is out of the seven?" This certainly implies more than one; and what other way can you make chapter 13 and chapter 17 make sense? Look at what it says at the beginning of verse 9 where the explanation begins: "Here is the mind which has wisdom." Every commentator I have ever heard believes the Roman Prince of Daniel 9:27 is the beast; this is a half truth. The other half of the story is given to us in Revelation, chapter 17.

In closing this chapter I would go back and emphasize what was said in two previous chapters. In Daniel, chapter 9, verse 27 which deals with the Roman Prince and the antichrist the KJV uses the pronoun "he" twice in this verse indicating the Roman Prince and the Antichrist are one and the same person. Later translators have changed this; the word "one" is substituted in the NKJV for the word "he" making the verse speak of two people. In 2ⁿᵈ Thessalonians 2:6 where Paul is speaking of the future antichrist he says "you know what is restraining that he may be revealed in his own time." It is not "who" is restraining but "what." As the devil will be restrained for 1,000 years in the bottomless pit, so the future antichrist is now being restrained in that same place. Notice two verses telling us this from the book of Revelation:

> Rev. 11:17 ".....the beast that ascends out of the bottomless pit will make war against them ...."

That verse introduced us to him.

> Rev. 17:8 "The beast that you saw was, and is not, and will ascend out of the bottomless pit and go to perdition."

I have again emphasized these points realizing the radical difference between the view given here and the view that is the accepted one.

A final point concerning the miracle working deceptive acts of the beast and the false prophet as recorded in the 13ᵗʰ chapter of Revelation. Although many miraculous signs are performed by these two are three major ones recorded; making fire come down from heaven (Elijah's miracle), the resurrection of the beast from the dead (Christ's miracle), and finally the creation of life (Genesis 1 & 2). In Genesis 2:7 "God formed man of the dust of the ground, and breathed into his nostrils the breath of life." In Revelation 13:14 & 15 men are commanded to make an image to the beast, and the false prophet "was granted power to give breath to the image of the beast." No wonder men will be deceived!"

CHAPTER 13

DANIEL'S 70TH WEEK

D aniel's 70th week is a cornerstone of end times prophecy found in one verse - Daniel 9:27. it has been stated twice in this book that the KJV translation of this verse is misleading causing readers to think that the Roman Prince of the first part is the antichrist of the second part. Later translators have changed this. Though the "week" itself is only mentioned here, most of the book of Revelations is devoted to this period of time - chapter 6 through 19 - or at least a portion of that period. Many other portions of Scripture deal with this time period also. The word translated "week" really means seven, a seven year period; the total time period would be 84 months of 30 days each, or 2,520 days. The last half of this period would be 42 months or 1,260 days; this is the period which occupies much of prophetic study. The accepted view is that this is one continuous period of beginning either with the appearance of the antichrist or with the invasion of Israel by Gog and Magog; there are differing opinions here. As the reader knows from reading a previous chapter of this book, I do not believe the Gog and Magog invasion occurs at this time The reasoning behind the view that the week starts with the appearance of antichrist goes like this. It can be easily demonstrated from Scripture that the desecration of the temple (abomination of desolation) takes place in the middle of the week. Prior to this the conquests of the antichrist take place; the first four seals of Revelation 6 or, paralleling this, are verses 4 - 8 of the Olivet discourse in Matthre 24 (abomination of desolation mentioned in verse 15). These conquests are also detailed in Daniel 11, verses 36 to 45 the antichrist apparently takes up residence in Jerusalem. Since the abomination of desolation takes place in the middle of the week and the conquests of antichrist occur before this; it then appears that the conquests take place in the first half of the week.this would be perfect reasoning except for one thing; an assumption is made that the 70th week is one continuous period. I would like to show that for our prophetic scenario be a logical, complete picture without contradictions, with all parts fitting together, this assumption cannot be correct.

Consider Daniel 9:27 for example. We are told that a covenant will be confirmed (enforced) for one week but that the sacrifices and offerings will be stopped in the middle of the week, possibly, or probably, canceling the covenant. If the standard view is correct the first half of this period will be a period of wars and associated calamities, with the one who is enforcing this covenant being the same one who is the cause of all these wars, and probably some of the nations involved in the covenant are being fought against by this person who is supposed to be the enforces of the covenant. Also, in Daniel 11 where we read about these apocalyptic wars, we read in verse 41 "He shall also enter the Glorious Land, and many countries shall be overthrown......" Will he enter the Glorious Land as friend or foe? It certainly appears from the context he is on a mission of conquest. His complete take over of Israel is given in verse 45 which would be at the midpoint of the week.

What will be the time when men will be saying "peace and safety?" Doesn't it seem likely it will be the same time when the covenant (of peace) will be enforced in the middle east? How could it be before then? The middle east seems to be the very source of our problems.

Consider the harlot of Revelation, chapters 17 & 18. It certainly looks like the time of "peace and safety" will coincide with the time the harlot is ruling (not militarily) over the kings of the earth. Chapter 17 tells us clearly this is the time just before the beast (antichrist) comes to power; in fact, he is given his power for the express purpose of destroying the harlot. If this is the beginning of the week then Israel would be agreeing to a covenant with the newly empowered antichrist, not a Roman Prince. Why would the nations think a person who would destroy this institution, which was so highly favored by them, would be the one to bring peace to the middle east. Instead, it seems likely this would trigger the conflicts that will follow. Remember that Daniel 9:27 says a Roman Prince will cause the sacrifices and offerings to cease. This brings us to another point. Will a masquerading Roman Prince declaring war with much of the world not be seen for what he is until the middle of the week, when he sits in the Temple of God declaring himself to be god? Not according to Daniel 11.

> Dan. 11:36 "Then the king shall do according to his own will; he shall exalt and magnify himself above every god, shall speak blasphemies against the god of gods ......"

> Dan. 11:37 "He shall regard neither the God of his fathers not the desire of women, nor regard any god; for he shall magnify himself above them all."

These were things he did at the very beginning of his conquests.

In the books of Daniel and Revelation the expressions "time, times, and half a time." "forty-two months." and "1,260 days" are mentioned seven times, always referring to the last half of the 70th week. Some would disagree with me on the 11th chapter of Revelation but a careful reading of verses 14 and 15 will indicate this is so. There is not one instance in Scripture of things happening in the first 1,260 days or in the course of the entire 70th week. As stated before only Daniel 9:27 mentions the 70th week and there describes a covenant made for that length of time but then is apparently broken in the middle of that period. The remainder of that verse describes the last half of the week but no mention is made of the wars of conquest which precede this last half. There is another verse in the 12th chapter of Daniel, verse 11, which, although it mentions 1,290 days (30 more days probably to Armageddon) is worth considering.

> Dan. 12:11 "And from the time that the daily sacrifice is taken away, and the abomination of desolation is set up, there shall be one thousand two hundred and ninety days."

One might take this to mean that the day the daily sacrifice is taken away, and the day the abomination of desolation is set up are one and the same day. Both of these events are found in Daniel 9:27 (Dan. 11:31 speaks of another similar event at another time in history). Dan. 11:45 speaks of the time when the antichrist will "plant the tents of his palace between the seas and the glorious holy mountain." an apparent reference to the time when he will take his place in the temple declaring himself to be God. Notice, however, in verse 41, as part of the description of his conquests, "He shall also enter the Glorious Land, and many countries shall be overthrown." It does not seem logical that he would do this while still enforcing a covenant of peace between Israel and her neighbors.

While placing a short, indeterminate, time period (the four horsemen of the Apocalypse) between the two halves of the 70th week may not make much of a difference in our over all picture of end time events, I believe it is a more sensible approach. In fact I will attempt to show in a later chapter that more time than this will be required because of certain other verses dealing with the subject. A time period between the wars and rumors of wars and the last 3 1/2 years is necessary.

CHAPTER 14

THE OLIVET DISCOURSE

Other than the books of Daniel and Revelation the Olivet Discourse is a main source of information on end time events. It is found in Matthew 24 and 25, Mark 13, Luke 21 and also Luke 17 although the discourse in Luke 17 did not take place on the Mount of Olives but the subject is much the same. There are also a few verses in Matthew 10 which deal with this subject. The Matthew and Luke accounts are the ones most often used. There is considerable agreement among commentators on these passages but there are also some passages which are difficult to interpret in their context. As with other prophetic passages we must always keep an eye on the book of Revelation which is always our guide in interpreting other portions. It is important also, as we shall see later, to compare the various Gospel accounts. There is no strict chronological order in these accounts but they move back and forth in time (as does the book of Revelation). The Matthew account pertains strictly to end time events but Luke makes clear cut distinctions between the apostolic age and the end time. Much confusion will be avoided if we realize the disciples asked two question of the Lord, which, in their minds at the time, all pertained to the same period of time. The first question, "Tell us, when will these things be?" and the second question, "And what will be sign of Your coming, and of the end of the age?" (Matt. 24:3). Although the Holy Spirit brought this to their remembrance, as promised, yet it appears they did not understand this discourse at the time; or why did they ask the Lord the question, "Lord, will You at this time restore the kingdom to Israel?" (Acts 1:6). The information is all there but to sort it out we must compare Gospel with Gospel and Scripture with Scripture. John's Gospel makes no reference to the Olivet Discourse or its content for John wrote after the destruction of the temple in 70AD. The first of the two questions asked by the disciples ("when will these things be?) had been answered by then, for this question pertained to the predicted destruction of the temple. John had a different message altogether, as recorded in those well known verses of John 14:1 - 3, which speak of the rapture. John later went on to give us Revelation, a full length description of end time events.

In Matthew verses 5 through 14 are in chronological order taking us to the end of Daniel's 70th week. Beginning in verse 15 we go back in time to the middle of the week and move forward again up to verse 30. verse 6 - 8 are parallel to the first four seals of Revelation 6; verses 9 - 12 appear to parallel the fifth seal as do verses 21 and 22. Verse 29 parallels the sixth seal, after that the discourse completely skips past the trumpet and bowl judgments of Revelation and goes right to Armageddon. The trumpet and bowl judgments do not appear to be in any of the Gospel accounts. Those very familiar with prophecy may have noticed a point made here, i.e. the great tribulation of verse 21 (which I believe is the same as that of verse 9) is the fifth seal and not a 3 1/2 period, and is terminated by the sixth seal of verse 29. Carefully compare these verses with those of Revelation 6 and see the exact parallel between the two. Some commentators think the fifth seal (great tribulation) pertains only to the persecution of the saints because of the emphasis in Revelation 6 and here in Matthew 24 on this very thing. We have been told in the scriptures that it should not surprise us to realize the world hates us. This does not mean that every person on earth hates us, but there is often a feeling of resentment, perhaps bitterness toward us, because the Gospel separates men. When the world degenerates into a state of complete lawlessness, where men hate each other, their hatred of the saints will intensify much more.

A few excerpts from these passages:

Matt. 24:10 "And then many will be offended, will betray one another, and will hate one another."

Matt. 24:12 "And because lawlessness will abound, the love of many will grow cold."

Matt. 24:21 "For then there will be great tribulation, such as has not been since the beginning of the world until this time, no, nor ever shall be."

Matt. 24:22 "And unless those days were shortened no flesh would be saved ......"

From Daniel a parallel passage:

Dan. 12:1 "......And there shall be a time of trouble, such as never was since there was a nation even to that time ...."

In 2 Thessalonians 2:6 - 8, the passage referred to in an earlier chapter, speaks of "lawlessness: and the "lawless one." Apparently the appearance of "lawlessness" and "the lawless one" occur at the same time; that would be at the time of the fifth seal which is the beginning of the last half of Daniel's 70th week. How does this compare with the United Nations and the "brotherhood of man" philosophy? I have heard commentators say that when the antichrist takes over there will be rejoicing and unity under his leadership. It doesn't look that way to me; he may be ruling over them but it will be a terrible time on earth. We should remember that he is responsible for the deaths of at least one quarter of the earth's inhabitant. and he is a ruthless dictator demanding worship. It's true that the world marvels at him because he has come back from the dead and is capable of miracles, but the judgments of God start falling on them not long after he comes to power. His government seems to completely tolerate lawlessness, and why not, he is the lawless one! No doubt, some will be glad to see him come to power, but their elation will be short lived.

In the Matthew account there are three separate warnings involving seven verses concerning false prophets and false christs. There is no mention of these anywhere else; the other prophetic Scriptures are concerned with the main characters and events of the prophetic picture. The saints of that future day are warned to take heed that no one deceives them. Yet, verse 24 appears to say that the elect cannot be deceived. Apparently there will be some non-Christian Christians in that day who, because of the perils of the time, will be looking for Christ to return and will be deceived into following false christs. Will they refuse the mark of the beast, be persecuted; is Satan's kingdom divided? It will be like today; many false religions used to deceive the nations. Although worship of the beast and his image will be the dominant religion there will still be many others who will be worshiping idols, following false christs described in Matthew 25, there will be those who seem to have a knowledge of Christianity but don't follow its precepts. I suspect the western nations, separated from the continents of Europe, Asia, and Africa by 3,000 miles of water will not be as subject to the military problems as those living in the areas of greatest conflict. I believe, though, that lawlessness will be world wide as described in the fifth seal. We read in prophecy about the north, the east and the south, but never the west.

I see a problem area in verses 29 and 30 of Matthew 24; the similar portion in Mark 13:24 - 26 appears to be much the same. These verses parallel the sixth seal of Revelation 6, which also presents us with the same problem.

Matt. 24:29 & 30 "Immediately after the tribulation of those days the sun will be darkened, and the moon will not give its light; the stars will fall from heaven, and the powers of the heavens will be shaken. Then the sign of the Son of Man will appear in heaven, and then all the tribes of the earth will mourn, and they will see the Son of Man coming on the clouds of heaven with power and great glory"

> Rev. 6:12 - 17 "I looked when He opened the sixth seal, and behold, there was a great earthquake; and the sun became black as sackcloth of hair, and the moon became like blood. And the stars of heaven fell to the earth, as a fig tree drops its late figs when it is shaken by a mighty wind. Then the sky receded as a scroll when it is rolled up, and every mountain and island was moved out of its place. And the kings of the earth, the great men, the rich men, the commanders, the mighty men, every slave and every free man, hid themselves in the caves and in the rocks of the mountains, and said to the mountains and rocks, 'Fall on us and hide us from the face of Him who sits on the throne and from the wrath of the Lamb! For the great day of His wrath has come, and who is able to stand?'"

There is considerable parallelism between the discourse in Matthew 24 and the six seals of Revelation 6. Mark's Gospel does not have the same degree of parallelism with Revelation 6 but it does have the events of the sixth seal following the great tribulation which is the fifth seal. It has been stated before that the trumpet and bowl judgments are not found in the Olivet discourse (or anywhere else). If the seals, trumpets and bowls of Revelation are in the sequence shown with the return of Christ at the end of these judgments, then we have a problem with the sixth seal. If men are enabled to see into heaven, in some way that doesn't destroy them, and immediately become aware of the throne of God and the wrath of the Lamb, this is apparently the time of Christ's coming. "The great day of His wrath has come" is evidently the time when "they will see the Son of Man coming on the clouds of heaven with power and great glory." The time when they will see into heaven should be equated with "the sign of the Son of Man will appear in heaven" for "then all the tribes of the earth will mourn" equates with men hiding "themselves in the caves and in the rocks of the mountains, and said to the mountains and rocks, 'Fall on us and hide us from the face of Him who sits on the throne and from the wrath of the Lamb!" Apparently the great destruction of the sixth seal causes a massive change in the earth's surface. It seems that the end of the sixth seal the return of Christ occurs, so where do we fit in the trumpet and bowl judgments? Also, the judgments in Revelation, generally speaking, increase in severity as they progress. Why would partial contamination and destruction of the waters and vegetation come after the sixth seal? How could mankind, after their experience of hiding in holes in the ground because of the wrath of the Lamb, possibly make such a come back as described in Revelation 11, where, after the death of the two witnesses, have a world wide Christmas style celebration at the time the sixth trumpet is about to sound? Consider the following:

> Rev. 9:20 "But the rest of mankind, who were not killed by these plagues, did not repent of the works of their hands, that they should not worship demons, and idols of gold, silver, brass, stone, and wood, which can neither see nor hear nor walk."

It is possible for irrational men after experiencing the trumpet judgments to still be idolaters, but how could men who looked up into heaven and, somehow, becoming completely aware of the throne of God and the coming of the wrath of the Lamb, still persist in idolatry?

All three synoptic Gospels have in almost the same words "the powers in heaven will be shaken," followed by either "the sign of the Son of Man "appearing in heaven or they "see the Son of Man coming." In Matthew and Mark the statement "the powers in heaven will be shaken" is preceded by "the stats of heaven will fall;" but in Luke we have some added information inserted in between these two statements.

> Luke 21:25 & 26 "…..sings …in the stars; and on the earth distress of nations, with perplexity, the sea and the waves roaring; men's hearts failing them from fear and the expectation of those things which are coming on the earth, for the powers of heaven will be shaken."

In Matthew and Mark the connecting word between the "stars" and the "powers" in "being shaken" is the word "and" but in Luke between the mention of the stars and the powers of heaven shaking we have the added information concerning things happening on earth, and then we have the connecting word "for" joining the happenings on earth with the powers of heaven shaking. Therefore, in Matthew and Mark the shaking of the heavenly powers is an added event to the cosmic disturbances, but in Luke the shaking of the heavenly powers appears to be the cause of the earthly catastrophes. If this is so I believe two observations should be made here. First, the earthly catastrophes of Luke's Gospel should be equated with the trumpet and bowl judgments; and, second, the sixth seal in Revelation not only starts the direct intervening judgment hand of God but also takes us to the consummation of God's judgments on earth. This means the trumpet and bowl judgments are to be placed inside the fifth seal judgment. One might wonder how the shaking of the powers in heaven could cause these earthly judgments but a casual reading of these judgments indicates the angels are the ones causing them; they blow the trumpets, judgment follows, they pour out the bowls and again judgment follows. There is something more to this than just pictorial language; we may have to wait for further illumination or for eternity to fully understand this. (How did the word of God create the universe? The words that Christ speaks are spirit and life; how can this be?) I offer this as an explanation for the missing trumpet and bowl judgments and why the coming of Christ occurs at the end of the sixth seal.

Another problem text for some is found in Matthew 24:

> Matt. 24:34 'Assuredly, I say to you, this generation will be no means pass away till all these things are fulfilled."

During this entire discourse Christ spoke to His disciples as though they were the ones who would go through this period and be present when Christ returned to establish His kingdom. It would not be proper to change the tense of the discourse for this one statement; it would leave the disciples in a state of bewilderment. I believe this is one of the reasons for the apparent belief in the imminency in the early church, and it took many decades for this attitude to change.

Further along in Matthew 24 we read:

> Matt. 24:37 "But as the days of Noah were, so also will the coming of the Son of Man be."

We must think of the "coming" referred to here as being the coming of Christ at Armageddon. Consider the verse which follows::

> Matt. 24:38 "For as in the days before the blood, they were eating and drinking, marrying and giving in marriage, until the day that Noah entered the ark."

This indicates life as usual with no expectation at all of an impending judgment. Certainly there will be no life as usual conditions just before the return of Christ; very little knowledge of Revelation is necessary to realize this is not possible. Either the "coming" includes the many judgments or we must insert a time span here between the condition mentioned and the great tribulation appears to be the time of "peace and safety."

Two other verses in Matthew 24 have been the subject of much controversy:

> Matt. 24:40 & 41 "Then two men will be in the field; one will be taken and the other left. Two women will be grinding at the mill; one will be taken and the other left."

Parallel passages to this are not found in Mark but are found in the 17th chapter of Luke. Two explanations have been offered for this. First, some say it refers to the rapture; the saved one will be taken and the unsaved one will be left. Perhaps something similar to this will happen at the time of the rapture. The second view is that one person is taken in judgment and the other left to go into the kingdom age. Those who hold to the second view quote from Luke 17:

> Luke 17:37 "And they answered and said to Him, 'Where, Lord?' So He said to them, 'Wherever the body is, there the eagles will be gathered together.'"

The answer to the disciples question about where the persons taken. Will be taken to, indicated they will die, and their bodies will be posed on the ground in some unknown place. My question to them is: what corroborating Biblical text is there to verify this view? The Biblical descriptions of the end time judgment is one of massive destruction and slaughter such as at Armageddon or around the world due to great earthquakes, huge hailstones, or even the Jewish people rising up against their enemies (Micah 5:7 -9). Those remaining will be gathered together for the judgment of the nations (Matt. 25:31 - 46). I respectfully disagree with both views. May I raise a question for my readers: "Who is doing the taking?"

Everyone says Christ is doing the taking, either at the rapture or at His second coming. I would like to offer a different explanation; it is the forces of Antichrist who are doing the taking, and it is occurring in Jerusalem and Judea at the time antichrist and his forces come into the temple and he declares himself to be God (abomination of desolation). If one is taken and one is left that means half of the people will be taken. Consider the following:

> Zech. 14:1 & 2 "Behold, the day of the Lord is coming, and your spoil will be divided in your midst, for I will gather all the nations to battle against Jerusalem; the city shall be taken, the houses rifled, and the women ravished. Half of the city shall go into captivity, but the remnant of the people shall not be cut off from the city."

In chapter 4 (Petra) I showed how the invasion of chapter 14 had to be at the middle of the 70th week and chapter described the invasion at the end (Armageddon). This is a continuation of the last two verses of chapter 13 which tells of a total of two thirds of the people being cut off and dying; but the initial removal of one half of the people is described here. I would like to present proof of this by comparing two Gospel accounts - Matthew 24 and Luke 17. In mathematics we say, things equal to the same thing are equal to each other, but in our study of prophecy we should say, things associated with the same thing are associated with each other. In Matthew 24 I would like to show an association of verse 34 - 36 (paralleling universes 17 and 18 in Matthew) with verse 31. This would then show an association between Matt. 24:15 and Luke 17:34 - 36.

> Matt. 24:15 "Therefore when you see the abomination of desolation spoken of by Daniel the Prophet, standing in the holy place ......"

Matt. 24:17 & 18 "Let him who is on the housetop not come down to take anything out of his house, and let him who is in the field not go back to get his clothes."

Luke 17:31 :In that day, he who is on the housetop, and his goods are in the house , let him not come down to take them away. And likewise the one who is in the field, let him not turn back."

Luke 17:34 - 36 "I tell you, in that night there will be two men in one bed, the one will be taken and the other will be left. Two women will be grinding together; the one will be taken and the other left. Two men will be in the field; the one will be taken and the other left."

Does this not show an association between Matthew 24:15 and Luke 17:34 - 36? The time when the abomination of desolation is seen is the time when the forces of antichrist invade Jerusalem, and is the same time when "one will be taken and the other will be left."

In both Matthew and Luke this time when one is taken and another is left is connected with the comparison of the coming of Christ to the days of Noah. In the portion of the discourse dealing with the days of Noah the "coming" (a noun, an event) is quite obviously a somewhat extended period of time starting in the days when Noah was building the ark and extending to the extinction of all human life by the flood waters. The emphasis of this portion is the unexpectedness of the judgment which came upon all mankind. This idea of unexpected judgment is also a primary emphasis of the following verses concerning the taking of one and leaving another behind. I believe there are three times in the end time scenario when unexpected judgment comes upon certain ones. The first one would be when those who are saying "peace and safety" are caught unawares when "sudden destruction" comes at the time the first of the four horsemen of the Apocalypse appears. The second time would be described here, when the antichrist and his forces invade Jerusalem and some flee to the mountains while others are caught, being unaware of what was about to happen. The third time would be at the return of Christ which, although known to be very near, yet the actual day and hour was an unexpected time.

This last point deserves some discussion. In the parable of the ten virgins (Matthew 25) we read of the bridegroom being delayed (verse 5), and verse 6 says "And at midnight a cry was heard: 'Behold, the bridegroom is coming'". Why would anyone want to get married at midnight? The idea here is he was not expected to be that late so the five foolish virgins had not made preparations for such an unexpected event. In the previous parable of the faithful and evil servant says in his heart, "My master is delaying his coming." I believe these parables must apply to the rapture. Although the rapture has not been discussed. How does this fit with the description of events in the book one event after another with no time lapse between; but let's take a look at the sixth bowl described in Revelation 16. after the judgment of the fifth bowl we read:

> Rev. 16:12 1y6 "Then the sixth angel poured out his bowl on the great river Euphrates, and its water was dried up, so that the way of the kings from the east might be prepared. And I saw three unclean spirits like frogs coming out of the mouth of the dragon, out of the mouth of the beast, and out of the mouth of the false prophet, for they are spirits of demons, performing signs which go out to the kings of the earth and of the whole world, to gather them to the battle of the great day of God Almighty, 'Behold, I am coming as a thief, Blessed is he who watches, and keeps his garments, lest he walk naked and they see his shame.' And they gathered them together to the place called in Hebrew, Armageddon."

This bowl is not a bowl judgment but it is leading to the final judgment at Armageddon. A consideration of the events described here should make us realize it will take a little time to fulfill all the predictions. How many days will it take? No one knows, but certainly not very many. At this point in time many are expecting Christ to return (if there ever was a time to believe in imminency this would be that time) for they have been forewarned "So you also, when you see all these things know that he is near, at the very doors." (Matt. 24:33); but notice what Christ says "Behold, I am coming as a thief." Here we have again the idea of being prepared for the unexpected.

This bring us to another very important message, one I have never heard mentioned by anyone speaking on this subject. In this end time scenario there will be many looking for the return of Christ (the rapture) who will not be true believers. Does that sound strange? Consider the following: In the parable of the evil servant we read of the servant saying "My master is delaying his coming." In the parable of the 10 virgins where all are waiting for the bridegroom five of them were denied entrance. In the parable of the talents where again all are awaiting the return of their lord one is described as unprofitable and cast into outer darkness. Then there are the many who will follow those who come in His name (post rapture) saying "I am the Christ." There is a reward for those who genuinely look for the return of Christ but I wonder, in our own day, with all the discussion of prophecy just how many are genuine? Since I was a child I have heard people say, "These are the last days."

A final observation on the last portion of the account in the 21st chapter of Luke.

> Luke 21:34 - 36 "But take heed to yourselves, lest your hearts be weighed down with carousing, drunkenness, and cares of this life, and that Day come on you unexpectedly (start of great tribulation). For it will come as a snare on all those who dwell on the face of the whole earth. Watch, therefore, and pray always that you may be counted worthy to escape all these things

that will come to pass, and to stand before the Son of Man."

This warning is obviously intended for those living just before the events of Revelation 6 through 19. If the pretribulation view as commonly taught is true this warning wouldn't make any sense, for the saints would all be raptured just before the events of Revelation 6 through 19. I believe in a pre-70th week rapture and the first half of the 70th week will be a time of "peace and safety." Evidently there will be evangelized and some saves in that period. In fact, those words "escape all these things that will come to pass" eliminates all the rapture views for they all occur either just before, or sometime during, the time when all those things are coming to pass; hence the necessity for some time period between the rapture and the beginning of the period when all those things will come to pass.

We find a similar problem at the beginning of the Olivet discourse. Since the Lord is answering the disciples questions about the end time He speaks to them as if they would be the ones living at that time; although this will not be the case there will be a group of people, some saved, some not. to whom this discourse is addressed. Since this is the case consider the first portion of the discourse.

> Matt. 24:2 - 6 "......Take heed that no one deceives you, for many will come in My name, saying 'I am the Christ,' and will deceive many. And you will hear of wars and rumors of wars. See that you are not troubled, for all these things must come to pass, but the end is not yet.

The group of people to whom this is specifically addressed will be reading this before the "action" starts; this is evident because the future tense is used here. Again, we see the need for a period of time between the rapture, which remover all the saints from the earth, and the time when the events of this last period begin.

At this point I believe we should consider the nature of the seventy weeks of Daniel. Daniel 9:24 states "Seventy weeks are determined for you people and for your holy city." We are told in the ninth chapter of Daniel that there will be a covenant or treaty between Israel and her neighbors for 3 1/2 years; and after that there will be a time of "Jacob's trouble" for another 3 ½ years; the question before us is whether or not this is a continuous period. I don't believe it is.

CHAPTER 15

Summary - "The Tribulation Period:

In chapter 1 we had a majority view, as well as some minority views, of the so called "tribulation period." In this chapter I will attempt to put together a coherent picture of the 70th week of Daniel which I believe, includes, but is not limited to, the calamities of what has been called the tribulation period. I have already stated that I believe the first 3 1/2 years of Daniel's 70th week will be a time of "peace and safety," a time when the religious, commercial, harlot of Revelation 17 & 18 will be reigning. She will be seated upon (holding down) the ten kings of a reviving Roman Empire. At this time Israel will have a covenant (peace agreement) with her neighboring nations, which will be enforced by the Roman Prince referred to in Daniel 9:27. This prince (called "prince" in Daniel 9:27) is king number seven of Revelation 17:10, and will be assassinated at the end of this period of 3 1/2 years after he causes the sacrifices and offerings to cease at the rebuilt temple. This person will revive and, according to Revelation 13 will astonish those who witness this, but I went to great lengths to demonstrate that though the body is restored to life, the soul is that of one of the five kings "who have fallen" of Revelation 17:10. He will then be the beast of Revelation 13, the little born of Daniel 7, the willful king of Daniel 11, the antichrist of 1 John 2, and the man of sin of 2 Thessalonians 2.

At this point in time there will be a break between the first and second halves of the 70th week, a probably short but unknown period of time during which the wars of Daniel 11 and Revelation 6 will take place. In order for this to take place he will be given the authority of the ten kings of Revelation 17 and his first order of business will be to destroy the harlot described in that same chapter. Although he will enter the nation of Israel (according to Daniel 11:41) during the time of his conquests he will not take his seat in the temple of God declaring himself to be God until after his conquests are completed (Dan. 11:45). However, he does declare himself to be God during the time of his conquests as shown in Daniel 11. At this time the message to Israel is that they will be hearing of wars and rumors of wars, but they are not to be troubled by these things for these wars will be among the Gentile nations. The 70th week of Daniel concerns Israel, but these wars and rumors of wars are predominantly among the Gentile nations which should give us reason to believe there is a break between the two halves of Daniel's 70th week.

At this point I will come clean and say that I do not believe there is any such thing as a tribulation period. Standard teaching on this subject says the first half of the 70th week is a tribulation period and the second half is a period of great tribulation. My position is not so much pretribulation rapture as it is pre-70th week rapture. The standard teaching on this subject comes from two verses in Matthew 24; one is verse 9 which has the word "tribulation," and the second verse is 21 which has the words "great tribulation." A careful examination of these two verses will indicate they are both talking about the same period of time; verse 9 saying "they will deliver you up to tribulation" i.e. the saints, but verse 21 says "For then there will be great tribulation, such as has not been since the beginning of the world." Clearly this is the same as that period of time described in Revelation 6 known as the fifth seal, and is identified as such in chapter seven of Revelation. Verse in Matthew 24 follows the statement in verse 8 "All these are the beginning of sorrows," this would be after the wars and conquests of the preceding verses and parallels the four horsemen of the Apocalypse. It is pretty much agreed upon by most commentators of the pretribulation position that the antichrist comes to power at this point and it is then that persecution of the saints begins. Verse 21, which describes the "great tribulation" follows the setting up of the "abomination of desolation" of verse 15 which is the same period of time when the persecution of saints takes place as well as the time of total lawlessness under the lawless one.

In this book I take a radical departure from standard teaching in contending that in Daniel 9:27 there are two persons and two time periods described. The two persons are the Roman Prince in the first half and the antichrist in the second half. The two periods of time are the two halves of the 70th week which have a separation between them. Daniel 9:27 and Daniel 12:11 are parallel verse, both speaking of the stopping of the sacrifices and offerings, and the setting up of the abomination of desolation (but only Daniel 9:27 speaks of the first half of the week). In both verses the two events are connected by the word "and" (kai in the Septuagint) which can connect either two adjacent or two separated (in time) events. Here is the problem. Can a person known as a Roman Prince enforce a middle east peace treaty and, at the same time, this same person, claims to be God and is the cause of wars in, around, and beyond that area, with the result that more than one fourth of the world's population are killed? This is what is necessary if we are to believe in a continuous seven year period known as Daniel's 70th week.

After some thought on this matter it seemed to me we should give attention to some other ideas which, I think, will show more convincingly that there is a time gap between the two halves of the 70th week. In the book of Daniel there are two times in the prophetic picture when the sacrifices and offering will be stopped and an abomination set up in the temple. The first time involved the person of Antiochus Epiphanes who in 170 - 168BC stopped the sacrifices and set up an abomination in the temple. In the first instance I used two dates, 170 and 168BC, one for the stopping of the sacrifices and the other for the setting up of the abomination in the temple. My proof of this comes from the Apocryphal book of I Maccabees where the early chapters deal with the great difficulties the Jews had with the Syrian king Antiochus Epiphanes. Antiochus began his reign in the 137th year of the Grecian Empire which would be 176BC. Now consider the following:

> I Maccabees 1:20 - 22 "And Antiochus, after that he had smitten Egypt, returned in the hundred and forty and third year, and went up against Israel and Jerusalem with a great multitude, and entered presumptuously into the sanctuary, and took the golden altar, and the candlestick of the light; and all that pertained thereto, and the table of the shewbread, and the cups to pour withal, and the bowls, and the golden censers, and the veil, and the crowns, and the adorning of gold which was on the face of the temple, and he sealed it all off.

The 143rd year would be 170BC. From the description given we would have to conclude this was the time when the sacrifices were stopped; but now consider a later passage in this same chapter.

> I Maccabees 1:54 & 59; "And on the fifteenth day of Chisley, in the hundred and forty and fifth year, they built an abomination of desolation upon the altar, and in the cities of Judah on every side they build idol altars …….And on the five and twentieth day of the month they sacrificed upon the idol altar, which was upon the altar of God."

Notice there was a two year gap between the stopping of the sacrifices and the setting up of the abomination on the altar. Now look at the description in the book of Daniel of these two events.

> Dan. 11:31 "And forces shall be mustered by him, and they shall defile the sanctuary fortress; then they shall take away the daily sacrifice and place there the abomination of desolation."

Without extra Biblical information we might conclude that the taking away of the sacrifices and the placing of the abomination of desolation took place on the same day. Now look at another verse which described an identical event at the end of the age.

> Dan. 12:11 "And from the time that the daily sacrifice is taken away, and the abomination of desolation is set up, there shall be one thousand two hundred and ninety days."

The descriptions of these two verses are so nearly identical some have mistakenly considered them to be referring to the same event, but the context makes this impossible. The point is this; if the two verses speak in almost identical terms of the same kind of events why can't we allow for the same time gap in the two verses? But the case is even stronger for Dan. 12;11 having a gap since there are two persons involved here and only one in Dan. 11:31. Remember in a previous chapter we observed that later translations (after the KJV) appeared to show the there were two persons involved in Dan. 9:27; also in chapter 17 of the book of Revelation there are two more kings after the one representing ancient Rome. One would be the future Roman Prince who would confirm the covenant with Israel for 7 years but then stop the sacrifices after 3 1/2 years, and the eight king would be the antichrist. Add to this the fact that every time we read about the antichrist he is either involved in war, persecuting the saints, or desecrating the temple; some have mistakenly applied passages to him that really apply to Antiochus Epiphanes. I suggest the reader read again Dan. 11:36 - 45 where we are introduced to the antichrist and see if that could possibly be the same one described in the first half of Dan. 9:27 as a

Roman Prince enforcing a covenant of peace, for what is described in Daniel 11 precedes the last half of Daniel's 70th week.

Another idea previously dealt with should be revisited at this time. The seven heads of Revelation 17, which, we are told, are seven kings starting with a Babylonian king and coming down through the various kingdoms to Rome and then to revived Rome. In John's day there had been six of the seven kings with one in the future who would continue a short time. I believe that one in the future would be the Roman Prince of Daniel 9:27 who would rule for 3 1/2 years and confirm the peace at that time. With this view all the kings would be ruling in some part of the seventy weeks of Daniel; except Nebuchadnezzar who preceded the vision, and a Roman Caesar being the sixth; these all being in the first sixty nine weeks of Daniel's seventieth week. But who is the eighth king mentioned in Revelation 17? as stated in a previous chapter this king is said to be "out of" the seven. He is not the seventh king but he is out of them. If this be so then there must be two persons in Daniel 9:27.

To continue the scenario, after the wars, and the antichrist has become world ruler (none or less), has desecrate the temple, and the world has embarked on an unparalleled period of lawlessness, we also find the hand of God in the two witnesses of Revelation 11 who are untouchable proclaiming the coming kingdom. At this time many Jews who had been in Jerusalem and Judea had fled into a great valley made for them as the Mount of Olives was split at just about the same time as the abomination of desolation described in Matthew 24. The holy city will be trodden under foot for forty-two months by the nations. The time period variously described as "time, times and half a time." half of the week, "forty two months," "1,260 days" eight times in all, leaves no doubt as to its length. Except for a time of a peace contract being enforced in the middle east there is never any reference to the first half of this week. The length of time of the fifth seal (lawlessness and persecution) is unknown, but we are told that unless those days are shortened no one would survive.

I believe the trumpets and bowls (Great Tribulation) parallels the fifth seal.

> Rev. 11:15 "then the seventh angel sounded: And there were loud voices in heaven, saying, 'The kingdoms of this world have become the kingdoms of our Lord and of His Christ and He shall reign forever and ever!'"

> Rev. 11:17 "We give You thanks O Lord God Almighty, the One who is and who was and who is to come, because You have taken Your great power and reigned."

There are two short time periods to be added to the 1,260, 30 days making a new total of 1,290 days, 45 days more making a final total of 1,335 days. These are both mentioned at the end of Daniel's prophecy. It is thought by many that the 30 days covers the period of the bowl judgments and takes us to the battle of Armageddon. The next 45 days which will involve the judgment of the nations (Matthew 25) and perhaps some other similar judgments will take us to the establishment of the kingdom. Daniel 12:12 says: "Blessed is he who waits, and comes to the one thousand three hundred and thirty - five days." The resurrection of the just occurs just prior to the kingdom age. The kingdom age will run its 1,000 year course and at the end of that period Satan, who had been bound, will be loosed to deceive and gather many peoples from many nations to come against the nation of Israel. This is recorded in Revelation 20 and, I have stated before, I believe this battle is the same as the one described in Ezekiel, chapters 38 and 39.

CHAPTER 16

LAST DAYS AND ETERNITY

How many times have you heard someone say, "These are the last days?" There are many views being propagated today on this subject, many conflicting with others. For those who believe in imminency the last days have been around for centuries, but even many of them after looking at the world scene must come to the same conclusion, i.e., we appear to be nearing the end. There are two ways of looking at this, first, is the stage being set for events that are predicted for the last time period - the seventieth week of Daniel, and, second, can we see events unfolding that are predicted for the latter time of the church age? In the first case if we don't have the facts of prophecy right we will be sorely disappointed. There are many who believed (and many still do believe) that Russia is getting ready to invade Israel. What did they think when the Berlin wall came down? It was back about the year 1975 I realized this was not so and realized Russia would have to give up its goal of world domination; consequently I was greatly elated to see the things that happened in 1998. There are certain things that we all agree on, particularly relating to the nation, and even since they took control of Jerusalem. When I see the great need for an enforced peace treaty middle east between Israel and her neighbors it makes the end seem near; but at the same time, as I stated in an earlier chapter I believe there has to be another kingdom, or empire, to fulfill the requirements of Daniel 7 before the end can come. I also believe the war on terror will be resolved before the end so that men can say "peace and safety (security)," but they will be saying this, I believe, in the first half of the 70th week. Though we may not see the harlot of Revelation 17 and 18 in full bloom we probably will see the formative stages. How many days are in the "last days?"

The other side to this discussion relates to passages in the epistles relating to "latter times" or "last days." There are three of them which are given below.

I Timothy 4:1 - 5 "Latter times"

2 Timothy 3:1 - "Last days"

2 Peter 3:3 - 9 "Last of the days"

Is there a progression here? There are some who say the entire church age could be referred to as the last days. If that is so why don't the apostles Paul and Peter just warn and exhort in the present tense about these things instead of telling us they will be in the last days, and how could anyone take Peter's warning to be anything else but a last days warning?

There are a few verses used to give support to the idea that the church age are the last days.

Acts 2:16 & 17 "But this is what was spoken by the prophet Joel: 'And it shall come to pass in the last days, says God, that I will pour out My Spirit on all flesh ......,' "

This passage was treated in another chapter, but it should be sufficient to say that the real fulfillment of this prophecy will be in the millennium and what was experienced on the day of Pentecost was not the fulfillment of this prophecy but an example of "what was spoken by the prophet Joel." Another example:

> Heb. 1:2 "(God) has in these last days spoken to us by His Son ……"

A comparison with verse one which says God spoke in various times and in different ways to the fathers tells us we are in a different era in which God has now spoken to us by His Son. It is this different era which are the last days before the establishment of His kingdom. See also 1 Pet. 1:20. Another example::

> 1 John 2:18 "Little children, it is the last hour, and as you have heard that the Antichrist is coming, even now many antichrists have come, by which we know that it is the last hour."

If the entire church age is the last hour why would John say "many antichrists have come, by which we know that it is the last hour?" Heresies came into the early church causing defections (see verse 19), but why would an observation of this cause John to say "it is the last hour" if the entire church age is the last hour? It is now the last hour? 1.2 billion Muslims say God has no son (see verse 22). Another passage, perhaps more difficult from the epistle of James.

> James 5:1 - 6 "Come now, you rich, weep and howl for your miseries that are coming upon you! Your riches are corrupted, and your garments are moth-eaten, your gold and silver are corroded. And their corrosion will be a witness against you and will eat your flesh like fire. You have heaped up treasure in the last days. Indeed the wages of the laborers who mowed your fields, which you kept back by fraud, cry out; and the cries of the reapers have reached the ears of the Lord of Sabaoth.

> You have lived on the earth in pleasure and luxury; you have fattened your hearts as in a day of slaughter. You have condemned, you have murdered the just; he does not resist you."

Does the history of the first century record anything like this: wealthy men cheating their employees and murdering just men who do not resist them? Could this be prophetic? If we take this literally when will the corroded money of the wealthy be a witness against them and eat their flesh like fire? There are many end time judgments on individuals; wheat and tares, the dragnet (Matt. 13), ten virgins, parable of the talents, judgment of the nations (Matt 25), faithful and evil servants (Matt 24). Should this one from James be added to them? There could be prophetic conditions in the future which would allow wealthy men to do the things mentioned here. The cries of the reapers reaching the ears of the Lord of Sabaoth seem to tell us of impending judgment.

Let us check into the three passages of Scripture that definitely deal with last days.

> 1 Tim. 4:1 - 3 "Now the Spirit expressly says that in latter times some will depart from the faith, giving heed to deceiving spirits and doctrines of demons, speaking lies in hypocrisy, having their own conscience seared with a hot iron, forbidding to marry, and commanding to abstain from foods which God created to be received with thanksgiving by those who believe and know the truth."

Verses 4 & 5 tell us that all food is good for which we give thanks. Since this speaks of apostasy in the last days (of the church age) this is probably the beginning of what we read about in 2 Thes. 2:3. which tells us the day of the Lord will not come unless the apostasy comes first The departure from the faith appears to be the deceiving spirits can be considered occultic and doctrines of demons speaking through men with seared consciences can be considered cultic.

There was apostasy in the early church and the Scriptures declare apostates were not true believers.

> Heb. 10:38 & 39 "ow the just shall live by faith, but if anyone draws back, my soul has no pleasure in him. But, we are not of those who draw back to perdition, but of those who believe to the saving of the soul."

> 1 John 2:19 (speaking of antichrists) "They went out from us, but they were not of us, for if they had been of us, they would have continued with us; but they went out that they might be made manifest, that none of them were of us."

These scriptures clearly teach that true believers are not of them who draw back, and those who go out from us are not true believers.

The word translated "goods" in 1 Tim. 4:3 was originally rendered "meats" in the KJV and, though the word does have a broader meaning than just "meats," I think what is referred to here probably should be "meats." Of the four times the word (ktisma) is used in the New Testament it is always used of a living creature, never of vegetation. The eating of meat, or certain kinds of meat, has always been a religious topic. Hinduism forbids the eating of all meat; Catholicism used to forbid the eating of meat on Fridays; the early church had a problem with eating meat which may have been offered an idol; Israelite dietary laws forbid the eating of certain kinds of meat. Have you ever seen a bumper sticker which read "Love animals, don't eat them?" PETA) People for the ethical treatment of animals) opposes meat eating. Vegetarianism has gotten to be quite a fad with doctors warning people of hardening of the arteries from eating to much beef. After the flood God told Noah every creeping thing was given to him for meat, and we find cattle mentioned many times in the Bible. Those who advocate vegetarianism from any moral religious viewpoint are attributing evil to God Almighty; what is the penalty for this infinite crime? A second point made in this verse is "forbidding to marry." In this country there are millions of unmarried couples living together; some say they intend to marry sometime, others have no such desire. The minds of men and women are being conditioned for what is coming, the soon arrival of a sizeable, influential, cult "forbidding to marry and commanding to abstain from meats." "Marriage is honorable among all, and the bed undefiled; but fornicators and adulterers God will judge." (Heb. 13:4)

The next passage from 2 Timothy is more lengthy than the others.

> 2 Tim. 3:1 - 9 "But know this, that in the last days perilous times will come; for men will be lovers of themselves, lovers of money, boasters, proud, blasphemers, disobedient to parents, unthankful, unholy, unloving, unforgiving, slanderers, without self-control, brutal, despisers of good, traitors, headstrong, haughty, lovers of pleasure rather than lovers of God, having a form of godliness but denying its power. And from such people turn away! For of this sort are those who creep into households and make captives of gullible women loaded down with sins, led away by various lusts, always learning and never able to come to the knowledge of the truth. Now as Jannes and Jambres resisted Moses, so do these also resist the truth; men of corrupt minds, disapproved concerning the faith; but they will progress no further, for their folly will be manifest to all, as theirs also was."

Paul is telling us here that evil in the hearts of men can make life difficult for others. It is obvious that evil rulers cause wars, persecutions, take away freedoms, etc, so I don't think that is the issue here. I think degradation in society in general, and particularly among influential people would be the most likely interpretation the phrase "disobedient to parents" indicates some will be children, probably teenagers, while the term "traitors" would be applicable to a person in a more influential position. In our everyday lives we experience difficulties because of the evil activities of others, so it appears that this condition will accelerate during the last days and, probably, will consummate in the world wide experience of the great tribulation. It seems strange but they will have a form of godliness - but will deny its power. We are not told to love and evangelize them but "from such people turn away." I believe the Scriptures teach in several places that some people cross the line, or pass the point of no return in this life where repentance is no longer possible; that seems to be the case here. Our attitude toward the majority of people, whether friend or not, is to recognize the infinite, eternal value of their souls, even though they may offend us at times. Verse 6 tells us that from this group there are some who are preoccupied with sex; recent events seem to indicate we are heading in that direction. Verse 8 tells how these men resist the truth just as vigorously as Jannes and Jambres (Egyptian magicians) resisted Moses. There is a daily parade of men on radio and TV resisting obvious moral truth trying their best to deceive, as they themselves have been deceived. It would be difficult to write a commentary on this passage without referring to the number one enemy of Christianity in the western world - liberalism, in all its various forms. One could write a book listing all the various ideas and goals of the various manifestations of liberalism and show how they conflict with the Bible. Yet there are those in this movement who have a "form of godliness," i.e. they have some kind of religion in their lives. Indeed, a good description of religious liberalism would be "having a form of godliness but denying the power thereof." The next passage to be treated after this in 2 Peter would be a good description of the antireligious liberal. Since all their ideals are contrary to Scripture they are certainly "despisers of good" and they "resist the truth." Verse 9 comes to the rescue of

The earliest prophecies to be fulfilled will be all the prophecies of the "last days," the last ones to be fulfilled will relate to eternity. There is probably more agreement about the conditions of eternity than of any other aspect of prophecy; therefore it is not my intention to look for some differences in the views of evangelicals. Since the intention of this book has been to focus on certain areas where I differ with many prophetic views I will not do so in this section, but instead I will focus on what I believe are wrong attitudes, wrong emphases, which I believe have come out of changing attitudes of the 20th century. Emphasis has been placed on love, tolerance, victory over bad habits or addictions, and finding a new meaning in life. I recall one time at the end of a meeting at a rescue mission on a young man wanted to discuss some issues with me. I began to discuss eternal destinies and wanted to show him how they can be changed. He told me he was not interested in such things, but only what I could do for him now. I immediately told him I had nothing to offer him. I wonder how many evangelicals would agree with me? The old hymn "Rescue the perishing" seems to have lost its appeal to many evangelicals today. It's time to abandon new evangelicalism and return to Jonathan Edwards-ism. It is time for us to once again get the full realizatin that eternity lasts forever, and once again get the full realization that eternity lasts forever, and ever, and ever, and ever, and ever, and ever, and ever!! When a man gets saved he gets saved from eternal punishment. We are saved unto good works but from eternal grief, anger , pain, despair. You can't trick a man into getting saved through clever psychological techniques. Men must be made aware of the enormity of their crimes, crimes committed against an infinite God for which the punishment is infinite; the punishment matches the crimes. Likewise the value of the atoning sacrifice of Christ must be seen to be infinite because it takes the place of the infinite, eternal punishment of sinful men. Let us not make the Gospel finite!

CHAPTER 17

DIFFICULTIES AND POSSIBLE SOLUTIONS

Concerning the things which I have written, I realize there are certain areas of difficulties where arguments against the views presented here could be made, so I would like to address some of these difficulties in this chapter. I will treat the following five areas:

Ezekiel 38 & 39

Imminency

Joel

"Heads and horns"

Matthew 13

There are probably other areas with difficulties, but at the present time I feel compelled to make some more observations on these five.

Let's start by making a comparison of these two verses:

> Is. 18:23 "In that day there will be a highway from Egypt to Assyria, and the Assyrian will come into Egypt, and the Egyptian into Assyria, and the Egyptians will serve with the Assyrians."

> Ez. 39:11 "It will come to pass in that day that I will give God a burial place there in Israel. The valley of those who pass by east of the sea; and it will obstruct travelers, because there they will bury Gog, and all his multitude. Therefore they will call it the Valley of Hamon Gog."

This may be speculative, but could the valley of those who pass by east of the sea be part of the highway from Egypt to Assyria? Who are the travelers who will be detoured because of the burial of the corpses? Verse 13 says "Indeed all the people of the land will be burying them ...." If all the people of Israel are aware of this burial ground, and are involved in the burial process themselves, why would they be attempting to pass by that way? The highway from Egypt to Assyria will be constructed, or provided by God Himself, during the millennium thus making this battle at the end of the millennium.

There are certain verses in chapter 39 which are used to prove the 70th week theory of this battle. They are verses 7, 22, 23 - 29.

> Ez. 39:7 "So I will make My holy name known in the midst of My people Israel, and I will not let them profane My holy name anymore. Then the nations shall know that I am the Lord, the Holy One in Israel."

When will this happen? - not until the millennium (or after). The nations will certainly not recognize the Lord in the 70th week of Daniel. Verses 23 - 29 once more tell the story of Israel's disobedience and punishment and this time it is preceded by the statement "The Gentiles shall know that the house of Israel went into captivity for their inequity......." Now the Gentiles can clearly see that God defends His people when they are obeying Him.

> Ez. 39:22 "So the house of Israel shall know that I am the Lord their God from that day forward."

In a discussion with a friend one time I was told that this verse was the "clincher" proving that this battle occurred during the 70th week and was the time of Israel's conversion. Let's make a few comparisons; there are various reasons given why Israel and the nations "know" that God is the Lord and particularly the Lord of the nation of Israel. In Ez. 36:23 "the nations shall know that I am the Lord" when they see Israel has been regathered from the nations (verse 24). In Ez. 36:36 the nations recognize the God of Israel when they see the rebuilding of Israel's cities and their extensive agricultural progress. In Ez. 37:28 the nations "will know that I, the Lord sanctify Israel, when My sanctuary is in their midst forevermore." In Ez. 38:16 & 23 and 39:6 & 7 the nations now recognize the Lord because of the results of the battle. Likewise it can be said of Israel. In Ez. 36:38 in answer to Israel's prayer "the ruined cities shall be filled with flocks of men. Then they shall know that I am the Lord." Generally, their knowing that He is the Lord is attributed to their regathering and conversion; see Ez. 37:6, 13 & 14. In Ez. 39:22 knowing that He is the Lord is said to be the result of the victorious battle against Gog and Magog in which Israel had no part whatsoever. Israel's conversion ("cleansing") is definitely associated with its regathering. Some verses seem to indicate Israel is brought back to the land and then converted while other verses seem to indicate Israel is converted first and then restored to the land. I would like to say at this point that what we see today is definitely NOT the restoration spoken of in the book of Ezekiel. To understand this seeming contradiction let us look at the 20th chapter of Ezekiel.

Ez. 20:33 - 38 "'As I live," says the Lord God, 'surely with a mighty hand, with an outstretched arm, and with fury poured out, I will rule over you. I will bring you out from the peoples and gather you out of the countries where you are scattered with a mighty hand, with an outstretched arm, and with fury poured out. And I will bring you into the wilderness of the peoples, and there I will plead My case with your fathers in the wilderness of the land of Egypt, so I will plead My case with you,; says the Lord God. ' I will make you pass under the rod, and I will bring you into the bond of covenant; I will purge the rebels from among you, and those who transgress against Me; I will bring them out of the country where they shall not enter the land of Israel. Then you will know that I am the Lord.'"

Compare this with another familiar passage:

Zech. 12:10 "And I will pour on the house of David and on the inhabitants of Jerusalem the Spirit of grace and supplication; then they will look on Me whom they have pierced; they will mourn for Him as one mourns for his only son, and grieve for Him as one grieves for a firstborn."

The portion in Ezekiel tells of the regathering and conversion of those not in the land; the Zechariah portion tells of the conversion of those in the land. Notice a portion from each passage:

Ezekiel: "Face to face"

Zechariah "They will look on Me"

Is not this the way Israel will be converted - recognizing their Messiah - rather than because of the results of a battle where they appear to be already converted. Zech. 2:11 (a millennial passage) says "then you will know that the Lord of hosts has sent Me to you." (Recognition of the Messiah). Zech. 13:9 says they will be brought through the fire before knowing the Lord. Joel 2:27 says they will know the Lord at the end of the plague and never again be put to shame. In Zech 2:4 (a millennial passage) we read of Jerusalem being inhabited as towns without walls because of the multitude of men and livestock. Compare this with Ez. 38:11 & 12 where we read of a peaceful people dwelling without walls and who have acquired livestock and goods. In Ez. 28:26 in the kingdom age they will "dwell securely" the same words used in Ez. 38:11. In Ezekiel, chapter 38, before the battle, they are twice called "My people Israel," three times they are said to "dwell securely," three times they are said to have been "gathered from the nations." In chapter 39, during the battle they are referred to as "My people Israel," after the battle, they are said to again "dwell securely," and in verse 27 God has "brought them from the peoples" and "gathered them out of their enemies lands." The same conditions are seen to be in existence before, during, and after the battle. Israel must have wondered (as did the nations 38:13) what was happening when this enormous invasion occurred. This seems to be finale to history after which there will never again be any doubt about their complete protection by, and association with, their God; both Israel and the nations will be assured of this. In the first 39 chapters of Ezekiel there are recorded the words "you" or "they" "shall know that I am the Lord;" This is certainly the great doctrinal emphasis of these chapters. Many times this statement is connected with judgment, i.e., the nations, or nations, afflicted by God will, as a result of their punishment, then recognize that He is the Lord, with no indication given that they will experience salvation as a result. This recognition of the sovereignty of the God of Israel occurs at various times in man's history and will reach an all encompassing climax in the "latter days." The events of chapters 38 and 39 appear to be that future time when the nations are compelled to know Him, and even the nation of Israel, His people, become fully persuaded, never to doubt again, that He is the sovereign Lord. If this is the case then the events describe here cannot be followed by any period of tribulation, great tribulation, trumpet judgments, bowl judgments, armageddon, judgment of the nations, etc. It must be placed at the end of the millennium. The point being made here is that this is the climax of history when the knowledge of God as sovereign Lord becomes universally and totally accepted. There will be no more need for any more persuasion. This condition may have existed at the very beginning of the Messianic kingdom but, apparently, did not continue throughout the entire kingdom age. Another point that perhaps I did not deal with sufficiently is the fact that certain nations are mentioned in Ezekiel, whereas in Revelation 20 the nations in the four corners of the earth are mentioned. I pointed out in the previous chapter on Gog and Magog that "many peoples" accompany these nations but failed to make known that there are five references to these "many peoples;" they are Ez. 38:6, 9, 15, 22 and 39:4. finally, in summing up this argument we compare four verses of chapter 38-8, 11, 12 and 14 with three verses from chapter 39-26, 27 and 28 it becomes obvious that the conditions referred to as future in chapter 39 are spoken of in the present tense (in relation to the battle) in chapter 38. In this era of prophetic teaching and excitement the battle of Gog and Magog has become a focal point and many believe it refers to Russia and is almost imminent. This event, important as it is, has been overrated. By far the most important event(s) for Israel and the nations in regard to knowing the sovereignty of God s the two fold experience of Israel:

1. Disobedience, expulsion, judgment.

2. Repentance, mercy, regathering.

This is what is emphasized in the latter part of chapter 39. because of its importance it is reiterated again after the description of the battle. The point I am making is: these verses cannot possibly be teaching the regathering of the nation of Israel after the battle since the verses from chapter 38 clearly teach otherwise; they must therefore, be a reaffirming of this most important teaching about the significance of the scattering and subsequent regathering of the nation Israel.

Concerning imminency the apostles appeared to know they would not live to see the return of Christ. They probably didn't think this way at the beginning of their ministry ("I will come again and receive you unto myself" John 14:3), but as time went on there were evidences they realized that death was their destiny here. Peter knew he was going to die from the very beginning; Paul realized it near the end. With the statement made concerning John ("If I will that he remain till I come, what is that to you?" John 21:22) The other apostles must have realized they were not going to survive until the return of Christ. The following verse (John 21:23) corrects the wrong impression made that John would survive until the second coming and in so doing indicate that he would die also. The great commission. The building of the church, evangelism to be world wide, not just in the Roman Empire. Timothy was told to commit to faithful men the things he had been taught and they in turn would teach others. An enormous amount of evangelism and discipline had to be done. It is my view that the hope of the imminent return of Christ slowly changed, and rightly so; this is the year 2018. But, let me say that with the resurgence of prophetic interest, and with some pretty obvious latter time indicators, I believe there is again a rising hope that "we shall not all sleep" (1 Cor.. 15:51). One last thought on the matter of expectancy, or the last of it on the part unbelievers. We must distinguish between two expectancies for the saints of two different time periods, and just the opposite for the unsaved - three unexpected events with terrible consequences. For the saints some passages (there are several) exhorting them to be looking for the appearing of Christ for them (Rapture), but there are other passages encouraging the saints to be looking for the second coming of Christ to establish His kingdom.

1 Thes. 1:10 "And to wait for His Son from heaven. Whom He raised from the dead, even Jesus who delivers us from the wrath to come. (Rapture)

Mark 13:29 "So you also, when you see these things happening, know that it (or He) is near, at the very doors." (Second coming)

1 Thes. 5:2 & 3 "For you yourselves know perfectly that the day of the Lord so comes as a thief in the night. For when they say, 'Peace and safety,' then sudden destruction comes upon them ......" (Start of tribulation)

Rev. 16:15 "Behold, I am coming as a thief. Blessed is he who watches, an keeps his garments, lest he walk naked, and they see his shame." (Armageddon)

2 Peter 3:10 "But the day of the Lord will come as a thief in the night, in which the heavens will pass away with a great noise, and the elements will melt with fervent heat, both the earth and the works that are in it will be burned up." {End of time}

We must exercise care when applying verses like these.

Another issue I would like to deal with concerns my view of Joel, particularly the first three verses of chapter one. As you will recall, my view of this book is that Joel is not speaking to the people of his day, but these three verse make it appear that he is. One might say that we can find no place in Scripture where such a condition as set forth here exists. But I would beg to differ. Consider the Olivet discourse, particularly as recorded in Matthews' Gospel. In the entire narrative Christ is speaking to the disciples of things far into the future as though these things would happen to them. Then there is that problematic (to some) verse which says "Assuredly, I say to you, this generation will by no means pass away till all these things are fulfilled" (Matt. 24:34). It is obvious this discourse did not apply either to the disciples or their generation. Then there was the discussion of the timing of Joel 2:28 & 29 where God says He will pour out His spirit on all flesh. In Ez. 36:27 and 37:14 God says He will "put my Spirit" and in 39:29 "pour out my Spirit" on His people Israel at the time of their restoration and conversion at the end for the 70th week. Although the first half of Joel 2:28 says "all flesh" the rest of the verse as well as the next verse certainly indicate it specifically refers to Israel. Also, mention should be made of the last verse in the book There are some differences of opinion among translators; some say their (Israel's) blood will be avenged, others say they (Israel) will be cleansed of blood-guiltiness. Either view would appear to agree with the context. Verse 19 tells of the shedding of innocent blood on the land of Judah and verse 20 tells of Judah's blessing in the kingdom age and necessarily they would have to forgiven of their past sins for this to be true. In chapter 2 I subscribed to the second view, i.e., the view that Israel's sin of bloodguiltiness had been removed. The reason is as follows; there is such a thing as parallelism in verses of Scripture. In verse 19 Egypt and Edom will be a desolation because of their violence against Judah; in verse 21 the Lord dwells in Zion because Israel has been cleansed of their sin of bloodguiltiness. It would not be proper to say the Lord dwells in Zion because the Lord has avenged the blood of the children of Judah. Another distinctive and peculiar teaching, or perhaps we should say reporting events, in this book is, again, an absence of something we would expect to find, if this was a report of events that happened in the past. This peculiarity is quite noticeable in chapter 2, verses 12 through 27. Just as there was no mention of Israel's specific sin(s) i.e., until we get to the last verse in the book where the implication is clear, so in these verses we find no record of Israel's response to God's demands as given in these verses. Rather the narrative says the Lord may respond mercifully, will respond mercifully, has responded mercifully, and finally in verse 26 and 27 the statement "My people will never be put to shame" climaxes this section, a strange way indeed to write about past events. If this was a historical record then certainly there would be recorded here Israel's response to God's commands, and then the merciful response on God's part toward them; but such is not the case. This then is another evidence of the fact that this book is totally prophetic; not part of a record of past events and part future prophetic events.

The difference between the 7 headed, 10 horned dragon of Rev. 12 and the 7 headed, 10 horned beast of Rev. 13 is quite clear. The body of a dragon tells us it is the devil (Rev. 12:9), but the best of Rev. 13 (the antichrist) is obviously a man. The distinguishing characteristic of the body of the beast is its makeup of a combination of leopard, bear and lion (compared to a dragon) taken from the three beasts of Daniel 7 The remark was made in the chapter on Daniel 7 that these three kingdoms were different from the kingdoms represented by the seven heads avoiding a duplication, but not only that, they distinguish it from the 7 headed dragon of chapter 12 of Revelation, hence it would seem very unlikely they would also be represented by three of the seven heads. In other words, if the three empires which make up the body of the beast are also three of the heads not only of the beast but also of the dragon then these three empires would lose their distinguishing characteristics which cause the beast to differ from the dragon. Chapter 12 tells of the continual battle between the dragon and the woman (Israel). Chapter 13 has a different emphasis, the persecution of the saints, (usually not Israel) and global domination. The heads and horns are associated with Israel although there were conquests of Gentile nations as well in that area of the world. Another question now arises; can a head also be a horn? This would be a duplication, but is it justified? What about Greece, a major nation within the old Roman Empire? The collapsing image of Daniel 2 appears to show Greece as a separate (from Rome) empire being destroyed at the same time; but all these empires are in the same general area, but increasing in size as they moved westward. If the revived Roman Empire is slightly larger than the original it would engulf the preceding empires, hence when it collapses so will the others also. But we are faced with the distinct possibility that some of these heads will also be part of the ten horn coalition, but this may not necessarily be the case. There are not enough other nations in that area (Europe and the middle east) that this may not be necessary. I do not believe that the European Union nations will make up the ten kings for these kings representing ten nations are of two types represented by iron and clay, and it looks like the iron would be a monarchy as in most middle eastern nations, and the clay would be the democratic nations of Europe, and these two are not compatible. Since we know the identity of the seven heads but not the ten horns we cannot answer this question dogmatically.

Matthew 13 - There are seven parables given here, three pairs and one single. The pairs related to each other appear to be:

1. The wheat & tares - the dragnet.

2. The mustard seed - the leaven.

3. The treasure hid in the field - the pearl of great price.

The parable of the sower stands by itself. For our purposes only two parables will be considered, the wheat & tares and the dragnet. These two mention the end of the age, the others do not and they probably can be applied to the present age. The problem with these two parables (and one of them is explained for us) is this; what time period do we put them in? Both parables speak of the angels separating the good and bad at the end of the age.

CHAPTER 18

AN EXAMINATION
OF THE THESSALONIAN EPISTLES

There are three separate discourses on end time events in these epistles.

1. I Thes. 4:13 - 18 concerns the dead in Christ and the rapture.

2. I Thes 5:1 - 11 concerns end time events and our relationship to them.

3. 2 Thes. 2:1 - 17 concerns Thessalonian difficulties with the day of the Lord and how it relates to them (and to us).

Apparently the Thessalonian Christians were aware of what we call the rapture, i.e. the catching up of living Christians, but were not properly informed concerning the fate of those who had died in Christ. Seems like they must have thought the rapture was going to happen very soon and were taken by surprise when their loved ones died. Paul informed them that the dead in Christ would rise first and then the living saints would be caught up together with them to meet the Lord in the air. They are then told to comfort one another with those words. This is probably the most specific description of the rapture found in the New Testament.

Although the next discourse in the fifth chapter is primarily focused on end time events the rapture is still in focus here, and how it fits into the end time order of events. In the previous discussion the Apostle Paul addressed an issue where they were not completely informed (the resurrection of the dead and its relation to the rapture), but in this discussion he starts by saying. "But concerning the times and the seasons, brethren, you have no need that I should write to you." "Times" refers to duration and "seasons" to characteristics of a certain period. It looks like the Thessalonians were totally informed about end time events. It's interesting to note the Apostle Paul spent about two weeks evangelizing and teaching in Thessalonica. It is doubtful, though, that they knew the duration of the kingdom age (1,000 years) since this was not revealed until John wrote Revelation. Consider verses 2 and 3:

> 1 Thes. 5:2 & 3 "For you yourselves know perfectly that the day of the Lord so comes as a thief in the night. For when they say, 'Peace and safety! (security)' then sudden destruction comes upon them, as labor pains upon a pregnant woman. And they shall not escape."

Three points are made here concerning the day of the Lord.

1. It will be sudden and unexpected.

2. It will be destructive.

3. There will be no escape.

The implication is that prior to the day of the Lord there will be peace, security, no expectation of any change and, apparently, a self-sufficient, arrogant attitude which indicates this is a strictly human accomplishment I say that because of the judgment that follows.

It should be noted in verse three the words "they" and "them" are used a total of three times. The objects of this judgment are those who will be saying "peace and safety." Verse four then immediately says "but you, brethren, are not in darkness, so that this Day should overtake you as a thief." The discourse then continues describing the differences between sons of day and sons of night. But consider the implications of verses three and four. Verse four says that the day should not overtake them (us) as a thief. Does this mean the day (of the Lord) will overtake the saints, but not unexpectedly? If this could be the case (mid trib., prewrath, post trib, positions0 then sudden destruction will come upon us also (but not unexpected) and we shall not escape either. Then why are the words" they" and "them" used exclusively? Moving on further to verse eight we are told as sons of light and of the day to put on the breastplate of faith and love, and as a helmet, the hope of salvation. This helmet, the hope of salvation, is referring to the future tense of our salvation. Notice the difference between the sons of darkness who complacently anticipate nothing but are heading for judgment, and the sons of light who are looking expectantly for the consummation of their salvation. The reason for wearing the helmet of the hope of salvation is given in verse nine. "For God did not appoint us to wrath, but to obtain salvation ....." the obtaining salvation is then defined for us in the next verse, "Who died for us, that whether we wake or sleep, we should live together with Him." The words "wake or sleep" are definitely referring to the rapture as indicated in verses sixteen and seventeen of the previous chapter. The next verse then tells us "Therefore comfort each other ......" Is there any comfort in the other rapture view which have the saints going through part, or all of the day of the Lord?

The discourse in 2 Thessalonians, chapter two again deals with end time events but also includes the rapture; verse one make this clear. Their problem was, they had been confused in their thinking about the day of the Lord and thought it had already come because of false information they had been given.. A question should be raised here, why are they concerned? If the rapture occurs during or at the end of the day of the Lord they would have good reason to be upset. They are urged to not be deceived by false information, and then the Apostle reminds them of some of the prophetic teaching they had received from him. Verse three has had some interpretation problems.

> 2 Thes. 2:3 "Let no one deceive you by any means; for that Day will not come unless the falling away comes first, and the man of sin is revealed, the son of perdition."

The apostasy is said to come first. The word translated apostasy is thought by some to refer to the rapture since the meaning of the Greek word could be departure. The word is used only one other time in the New Testament and there it refers to a doctrinal departure, so I think the word apostasy is appropriate. 1 Tim. 4:1 tells us that in the last days some will depart from the faith. I believe the apostasy spoken of here will be the final state of that apostasy. The word "first" in this verse is important; it indicated the apostasy will occur before the day of the Lord. The man of sin, or lawlessness, is mentioned as being revealed. We know from other Scriptures, 1 Thessalonians included, that the day of the Lord commences with the revealing of the man of sin. Daniel 11 tells us the man of sin declares deity for himself early in his military conquests. Refer to a previous chapter for details on restraining. Verse 8 when compared with Rev. 19:20 looks like contradiction.

> 2 Thes. 2:8 "And then the lawless one will be revealed, whom the Lord will consume with the breath of His mouth, and destroy with the brightness of His coming."

> Rev. 19:20 "Then the beast was captured, and with him the false prophet ....These two were cast alive into the lake of fire burning with brimstone."

We must keep in mind that "this mortal must put on immortality (1 Cor. 15:530). This applies to the unsaved as well as the saved;

if not, they could not be punished eternally. Since 1 Thes. 2:8 tells us he will be destroyed and Rev, 19:20 says he will be cast alive into the lake of fire, and we know from Rev. 20:14 that the lake of fire will be the eternal abode of the resurrected unsaved, it follows then that the beast and false prophet are slain and resurrected at Armageddon and then cast alive (in their immortal bodies) into the lake of fire. The rest of the unsaved dead are resurrected after the millennium, judged at the great white throne judgment and are then also cast into the lake of fire. Apparently there is an in between state where the souls of men are tormented in hell (see Luke 16). Verses 9 through 12 tell of the deception and consequent condemnation of those who refused to believe the gospel, and verses 13 through 17 by contrast describe the salvation and obtaining of glory of the saints. In verse 15 the saints are admonished to stand fast and hold the traditions which they were taught and in verse 17 they are told God would comfort their hearts. There is nothing in this entire chapter that indicate the saints will go into the day of the Lord but rather the message seems to be"

1. The saints should not believe they are in the day of the Lord for,

2. That is the time when Antichrist will deceive those who refused the Gospel but,

3. They have believed the gospel and are called to obtain glory (not judgment) and God will comfort their hearts as they hold fast the traditions they were taught.

CHAPTER 19

OBSERVATIONS AND SPECULATIONS

I t is inevitable that those who become involved in prophecy will continually, carefully observe world events in hope of making a connection between Bible prophecy and current events. In my experience in this field I have read or listened to perhaps a hundred or more prophecy teachers, I noticed that nearly all made some connection between Bible prophecy and current events. I would like to deal with some of those issues now.

The U.N. has been associated with end time events, in particular the coming antichrist, who they think will take control of the U.N. to become a world ruler. This view does not agree with the Scriptures. In a previous chapter it was shown from Revelation, chapter 17, that the antichrist comes to power as a result of the ten kings of the reviving Roman Empire giving him their power for the purpose of destroying the harlot After this he begins his series of conquests. I fail to see the UN in prophecy.

Another issue is the European Union (EU). Many have equated the EU with the ten kings of the revived Roman Empire. This cannot be true either. There are more than ten members in the EU and they are democratic (to some degree) nations. But Daniel's image tells us the ten kings (toes) are part iron and clay. I believe, and many concur, that clay represents democratic governments and the iron represents monarchic or dictatorship governments. Since the Roman Empire included not just Europe but also the middle east and North Africa we must include countries from those areas also. In those areas we find the iron toes and in Europe the clay. We are told in Daniel these kings cannot join together, but in Revelation 17 they find common cause and untie the beast. If this is true then the attempt to democratize the Middle East will not succeed.

Another issue is Israel and, perhaps, this is the most important one. Most students of prophecy believe that what we see in Israel today (aliyah) is a fulfillment of prophecy. I believed this is not a fulfillment of prophecy but rather a preparation for the fulfillment of prophecy - a setting of the stage for future events I believe we are in that implied period of time between Daniel 9:26 and 9:27. Daniel 9:26 describes the wars and desolations in and around Jerusalem., and Daniel 9:27, without explanation, tells about a covenant between an Israel that ceased to exist in the previous verse, and some if its neighbors; in addition it mentions a restoration of temple sacrifices. Contrasted with this are many verses which tell of the return of the Jews to Israel at the end (or near the end) of Daniel's 70th week. This will be a supernatural event - the exact opposite of what we see today. When we read Ezekiel 37 (valley of dry bones) there is much evidence there to show the supernatural aspect of the return of the Jews to the land. Consider the following:

> Ez. 37:11 - 14 "Then He sais to me, 'Son of man these bones are the whole house of Israel. They indeed say, "Our bones are dry, our hope is lost, and we ourselves are cut off!"'Therefore prophesy and say to them, Thus says the Lord God; "'Behold, O My people, I will open your graves and cause you to come up from your graves, and bring you into the land of Israel. Then you shall know that I am the Lord, when I have opened your graves. I will put My Spirit in you, and you shall live,

and I will place you in your own land. Then you shall know that I, the Lord, have spoken it and performed it' says the Lord."

The return of Israel to the land is usually (perhaps always) associated with their conversion. Israel has been a nation for about 75 years now, and aliyah has been going on all these years, but there is no indication of any substantial conversion there. During that seventy-five years they have certainly not said, "Our hope has perished. We are completely cut off."

Then there is Gog and Magog (Russia they believe) that is often commented on in spite of what has happened to that nation. This has been dealt with in two previous chapters.

"The kings of the east" is often discussed; this, of course, refers to China and other allied nations from that area. Rev. 16:12 makes mention of the drying up of the Euphrates to prepare a way for the kings from the east. This is for the march to Armageddon. An error made here is the associating of the two hundred million "horsemen" with the "kings from the east." One is the seventh bowl judgment and refers to an army of men marching toward Armageddon. Reference is often made to the population of China and to the two hundred million mentioned in Rev. 8:16, but this is not valid.

Since the advent of terrorism (9- 1 - 1) there has been an emphasis on Islam. An Islamic beast theory has been put forth by some, others just see Islamic states cooperating with Russia in the Gog invasion. Islam started in the seventh century. Rev. 17:8 tells us the beast "was and is not" but will come back again. This means he existed some time before John lived and, therefore, probably a millennium before Mohammed came on the scene. He will be a former king who lived centuries before John and cannot possibly be an Islamic. As for myself, I have, in previous chapters, told of certain things I believe will come to pass in the near future, probably before the end of the church age. These include, discovery of Noah's ark, discovery of the ark of the covenant, a new empire arising in the far east, an influential cult arising forbidding to marry and to eat meat, many evil influential men with a heavy sexual appetite arising, the advance of liberalism both religious and nonreligious, the pushing back of terrorism, increasing ill will between certain European and middle eastern countries, and the United States. Time will tell.

Other things can be said and I have deliberately avoided expressing my views on two very controversial ideas. If this book ever finds its way into the market place of ideas there will be enough controversial material contained herein.

CHAPTER 20

THE COMING

The second coming of Christ has generally been considered a two phase event; first the rapture and then Armageddon. It has been a difficult position to make a satisfactory explanation for in the minds of many. It appears to be a second and third coming. Those who hold to either a pretrib or midtrib position sometimes do not refer to the rapture as the second coming, since Christ does not come to earth; but we are caught up to meet Him in the air., Those of the prewrath position (rapture at the end of the sixth seal) insist that Christ remains here during the remaining period of judgments, thus enabling them to believe in one second coming. Postrib people seem to have no problem with a single second coming.

The following is my view, I agree with those who would exclude the rapture from the second coming (a coming to earth, as Christ did the first time). It is absolutely to view things this way or we must have a second and third coming.

The message being conveyed in the context of Matt. 24:42 and 44 is one of severe warning to be alert, for something very threatening or upsetting may soon happen. It is a negative message and there is the continually mentioned idea that this will be unexpected. The parable of the thief breaking in is compared to the coming of Christ; it is unexpected This appears to be the opposite of verses pertaining to the rapture, where we are told to be looking eagerly and expectantly for Christ to come, and catch us up to be with Him; certainly not a negative message or warning..

There appears to be a succession of events described in Matt. 24:37 -44. They are:

1. The judgment of Noah's day - verses 37 - 39.

2. The judgment of "one taken and one left" - verses 40 -42.

3. The judgment of the unexpected coming as a thief (referring Christ's coming) - verses 43-33 - see also Rev. 16:15.

The judgement of Noah's day shows that people were caught totally unaware of what was coming. Surely, then, this must be referring to the coming judgment of Revelation, Chapters 6 through 19. This passage certainly parallels 1 Thes. 5:3 - "when they shall say peace and security then sudden destruction comes upon them as travail upon woman with child." I have stated previously that I believe there is a space of seven years (at least) between the rapture and the beginning of the judgments of the last 3 1/2 years.

Also I believe there will be a space of several years between the first 3 1/2 years and the last 3 1/2 years. Verse 40 says: "then two men will be in the field — but the word "then" does not mean immediately, or, as soon as the judgments begin, but rather during that period of judgments. There is the warning to flee when the "abomination of desolation" is reported to them. This is some time after the interruption of peace on the earth. The verses mentioning "one taken and the other left" refer to those who do not flee when they should.

There are two ways to look at verse 42 which says: "Watch therefore, for you do not know what hour your Lord is coming." Some relate the time of the Lord's coming to the time when one is taken and another is left; and consequently teach that one is taken in judgment (by Christ) and the other is not. I believe it has been demonstrated in a previous chapter that this event occurs at the time of the revealing of the "abomination of desolation," which would be the midpoint of the 70th week. I believe the correct way to look at this verse is to be ever watchful for things that will occur since we don't know when the Lord will return. A parallel portion in Luke. 22:4 - 36 gives us more insight, particularly in verse 36: "Watch therefore, and pray always that you may be counted worthy to escape all these things that will come pass, and to stand before the Son of Man."

Verse 43 and 44 then would apply to the actual return of Christ. The succession of events described in Matt. 24:37-44 seems to be.

1.   The judgment of Noah's day <u>represents</u> the starting to the point of the end time judgment.

2.   The "one taken and one left" judgment occurs at the middle of the 70th week."

3.   The judgment of <u>the unexpected</u> coming are at the same time.

The conclusion of the matter is this; verses like Matt. 24:42 and 44 bear no resemblance to those verses exhorting the saints to look for Christ to come to take them home. (rapture); rather they refer to the middle of the 70th week, and the other at the end of the 70th week.

A final word for those who hold to the partial rapture theory, and interpret some of these verses to mean that only those who are watching and ready will be raptured. That is not the intent of these verses; rather the message is to be watching, and ready for that (judgment) which is coming. If any church age saints missed the rapture they would not be at the marriage supper of the Lamb (and the church is his bride), nor would they be at the judgment seat of Christ, but "we must all appear before the judgment seat of Christ." (2Cor. 5:10.)

CHAPTER 21

RIGHTLY DIVIDING THE WORD
OF PROPHECY

First the rapture. Afterward much religious activity. Consider the following:

Matt. 7:22 and 23 - tells of the rejection of certain charismatic groups at the end of the age.

Matt. 13:37-43 - the wheat and tares parable described the real and false Christians at the rapture.

Matt. 13:47-50 - the drag net with both good fish and bad again describe the final end for both true and false Christians at the end of the age.

Matt. 24L45-51 - the parable of the good and evil household servant describes the final end for both the true and false servants (both relived in the second coming) (rapture).

Matt. 25:1-13 - the parable of the 10 virgins describes the acceptance of the wise and rejection of the foolish at the coming of the bridegroom (Christ). (Rapture)

Matt 25:14-30 - the parable of the servants called to handle their master's business describes the profitable and unprofitable servants when he returns. A reference to profitable and unprofitable "Christians" at the end of the age. (Rapture).

Matt. 25:31-46 - describes the sheep (saved) and goat (unsaved) nations (Gentiles) at the final judgment. Both appear to have been fully aware of the person of Christ an, no doubt, of His second coming. (Final end).

Matt. 24:5, 11, 23, 24, 25, 26 - false Christ's and false prophets indicating the renewed interest in the return of Christ.

Matt. 24:14 - the gospel of the kingdom will be preached world wide.

Rev. 6:9, 10, 11,; 7:9, 14 - a huge multitude of martyrs for Christ during the great tribulation.

Rev. 7:3-8 - the 144,000 sealed Jewish servants of God.

Rev. 11 - describes the two witnesses who become known world wide.

Rev. 14:6, 7 - an angel flying in heaven preaching to every tribe on earth.

Is the rule of antichrist really world wide? Babylon was called a world empire (Dan. 2:38) Darius the Mede considered his kingdom to be a world wide kingdom (Dan. 6:25.) Caesar gave an order for the whole world to be taxed (registered - Luke 2:1.) In Col. 1:6 Paul says the gospel has come to them, as it has also in all the world - was this true in Paul's day? In Daniel 11 the battles of the antichrist are never directed toward the west - 3,000 miles of water are still a barrier. The rule of antichrist may be world wide in a small way, but it can't be world wide with the same authority that Hitler or Stalin exercised in their controlled areas. The ward of nations I believe will extend to the western world, however, in order for one fourth of the world's population to be exterminated. Another idea to be considered is this; how much control over the populace can antichrist have (during that 42 months) when the judgments of the sixth seal and the seven trumpets are unleashed. We are told that the sixth seal judgment is poured out to save mankind from extinction, due to uncontrolled lawlessness. Then there are the kings (plural) of the east (Rev. 16:12), and the kings of the earth and the whole world (Rev. 16:14). How does the rule of antichrist fit with these condition? Why would demonic forces have to go world wide to the nation's leaders to persuade them to come to the battle of Armageddon, if the antichrist was the world ruler?

Other considerations follow. What about the 144,000 sealed, and the two witnesses which no one could harm, and who may have announced the coming judgments; at least they were able to inflict judgments on the earth as often as they desired. How long did the seas and fresh water supplies remain in a blood type condition? No one could survive on earth very long under those conditions. (The environmentalists will really lose their sanity when those judgments hit.) how long can cattle survive without grass? These are all questions that cause us to ask: how extensive and sovereign will the antichrist's rule be; and how extensive, severe and enduring will the judgments be? The judgment of the nations doesn't seem like these nations were under a hard rule by the antichrist. Even the goat nations appear to be surprised at their condemnation. It had nothing to do with the mark of the beast. Not caring for Christ's people is a hell deserving crime - infinite in dimension. Doing good is not an option - not doing any good is the infinite crime.

I cannot make my next point with those who think the rapture is in view in Matthew, chapters 24 and 25. the rapture was a mystery (sacred secret) until Paul later revealed it in his epistles. Why would there be conversation between Christ and false professing, believers at the rapture telling them of their condemnation. If we place the time at the end (just after armageddon) that would seem to make sense, but we have a problem with that also. When we look at the sequence of events in Revelation, some of which are described in the Olivet discourse, and then read verses such as:

> Matt. 24:45-51 (faithful and evil servant);
>
> Matt. 25:1-13 (10 virgins);
>
> Matt. 25:14-30 (the talents);
>
> Mark 13:32- 37 (the doorkeeper);

We begin to wonder if the extreme difficulties of this period as described in those portions (Revelation and Olivet Discourse) can apply to these parables, as well as to the nations involved in the judgment of the nations.

Consider the following:

> Matt. 24:48, 49, 50: "But if that evil servant says in his heart 'My master is delaying his coming,' and begins to beat his fellow servants, and to eat and drink with the drunkards, the master of that servant will come on a day when he is not looking for him —."

This portion is obviously referring to a professing, but unbelieving, "Christian." This is true of the other parables previously mentioned. Could a man react this way in a time like that described in Revelation, chapters 6 through 19? It makes one wonder if the entire world is affected the same way by these judgments. The western world, unknown in Biblical days, never seems to be referred to in prophecy. The location of mystery Babylon is not made known, but it is a huge commercial, coastal city (or cities - mega city): but the nations comprising the western world cannot be found in Scripture. Is it possible they be referred to be here in these parables? I know of at least one prophetic teacher who thinks the United States may be a sheep nation. We get the impression from reading the book of Revelation that the judgments are worldwide, but the question of severity arises when we read these parables (and others - wheat and tares, good fish and bad). It would seem likely that under the pressures of the Antichrist with the multitude of martyrs ((fifth seal), as well as the catastrophic judgements that follow that men would surely take one side or the other. How is it possible to have "evil servants," "foolish virgins," unprofitable servants," as well as goat nations? All of these people represented here are people who believed in the (eventual) second coming of Christ. This seems more like present day United Stated religious environment than one that will exist during the so called "great tribulation." It seems logical to me that some parts of the world will not be as severely tested and judged as other parts; and I would think that it would be the western world that will be the place where the fulfillment of these parables, as well as the judgment of the nations, would primarily be fulfilled/

Perhaps I can make the point a little more plain. Consider Luke 21:26 & 27:

> "Men's hearts failing them from fear and the expectation of those things which are coming on the earth, for the powers of heaven will be shaken. Then they will see the Son of Man coming in a cloud with power and great glory."

Compare this with the previous portion quoted from Matt. 24:48-50. Is it possible to have these two conditions at the same time and same place? (Doesn't anyone else recognize these problems, or am I a lone voice?)) They are obviously not in the same time period.

In Peter 3:4 a prophecy concerning the return of Christ at the end of the current (church) age indicates there will be much skepticism concerning the second coming. By way of contrast, after the rapture the second coming will be the main topic of conversation; even after the ascension to power of the antichrist. Just prior to the seal judgments there will be a time of peace and security, but even then apparently many will come to realize that the second coming is drawing near. There are a multitude of passages that indicate many know of the second coming along with the fact that the Kingdom Gospel will be preached in the whole world.

The second coming referred to in Peter's passage is referring to the destruction of the universe (II Pet. 3:10). The phrase "Day of the Lord" is used only for the beginning of the last 3 1/2 years and as here.

And though I have the gift of prophecy, and understand all mysteries and all knowledge, and though I have all faith, so that I could remove mountains, but have not love, I am nothing. 1 Cor. 13:2

A time of attempted rule by the antichrist and of terrible judgments by God—seven seals, trumpets and bowls, terminating in Armageddon—a return of Christ with his saints with a great destruction of life. Following this, a judgment of the nations and the establishment of the kingdom.

The year of this establishment is given in Hosea 5:13-14 and 6:1-2 its description is given in Ezekiel chapters 40-48.

The time from the start of Babylon the Great to the establishment of the kingdom will not be 7 years but somewhere between 20 and 25 years. The date for the establishment of the kingdom seems to be about 2070 AD. Second coming events should start somewhere between 2045-2050 AD.

In my book, I attempt to show the identity of the antichrist to be Antiochus Epiphanes and I am sure I will be criticized for two things: The date for the establishment of the kingdom and the identifying of the antichrist.

Praise the Lord
He's coming soon
Walt Madenford

CPSIA information can be obtained
at www.ICGtesting.com
Printed in the USA
FFHW020008200619
53120696-58765FF